LEARNING.
●●●●●●●●●●●●● **services**

01726 226784
learning.centre4@
st-austell.ac.uk

Cornwall College St Austell
Learning Centre – Level 4

This resource is to be returned on or before the last date stamped below. To renew items please contact the Centre

Three Week Loan

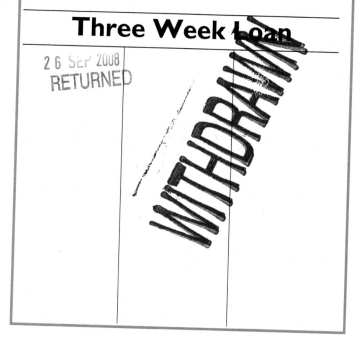

Studymates

25 Key Topics in Business Studies
25 Key Topics in Human Resources
25 Key Topics in Marketing
Accident & Emergency Nursing
Business Organisation
Cultural Studies
English Legal System
European Reformation
GCSE Chemistry
GCSE English
GCSE History: Schools History Project
GCSE Sciences
Genetics
Hitler & Nazi Germany
Land Law
Macroeconomics
Organic Chemistry
Practical Drama & Theatre Arts
Revolutionary Conflicts
Social Anthropology
Social Statistics
Speaking Better French
Speaking English
Studying Chaucer
Studying History
Studying Literature
Studying Poetry
Understanding Maths
Using Information Technology

Many other titles in preparation

Revolutionary Conflicts

Terrorism and Unconventional Warfare Explained

Richard Thackrah

www.studymates.co.uk

Typeset by PDQ Typesetting, Newcastle-under-Lyme, Staffordshire
Printed and bound in Great Britain by the Baskerville Press Ltd, Salisbury.

Contents

Preface

This work will be useful to students in further and adult tertiary education, the police, the military, practitioners in the field of countering terrorism and interested lay people.

I would like to thank Julie Aram of Tanimara Secretarial Services for her expert word processing skills, Graham Lawlor of Studymates for his support and advice and Peter Williams.

I wish to dedicate this work to all victims of revolutionary conflict around the globe.

Richard Thackrah
October 2001

1

The Nature of Revolutionary Conflict

One-minute summary – In this chapter you will learn about the nature of revolutionary conflict – its motivation, effects and forms. In particular we will explore:

▶ the nature of unconventional warfare
▶ civil wars
▶ religious conflicts
▶ guerrilla warfare theories and models: Guevara, Marighela, Debray
▶ the conflict spectrum
▶ conditions conducive to urban violence.

Revolutionary conflict

Revolutionary conflict or revolutionary terror is purely political. Revolutions are not by definition terrorist events! Indeed none have been successfully carried out without resort to terrorist tactics. It is increasingly difficult for an untrained and sparsely equipped indigenous army to wage a successful guerrilla war against a national standing army.

With mounting frustration in the face of insurmountable odds, it is increasingly easy to resort to terror-violence to achieve by psychological force what it is not possible to achieve by force of arms.

Revolutions have occurred throughout history without recourse to terror–violence, and there needs to be an effort made to understand why such revolutions do not continue to occur without the use of terrorist tactics.

Do they occur, or can they not occur successfully, without the use of terrorism? The legitimacy of a cause does not in itself legitimise the use of certain forms of violence against the terrorist. There are limits to the legitimate use of violence, regardless of the justice of the cause. A condemnation of terrorism is a reiteration of the limits of violence which a civilised society has decided to set. It does not in any sense preclude the right to revolution.

Do today's revolutionaries want to be guerrillas not terrorists? This is a moot point as there is no stigma attached to the status of rebels. Revolutions can still occur despite a ban on terrorist tactics. Most modern states have experienced a period of revolutionary violence, and a state has an obligation to restrain its use of violence against its citizens. The means to ensure law and order must be carefully balanced against the responsibility of the government to ensure the maximum protection of civil rights and liberties.

Sub-revolutionary politically motivated systematic terrorism is employed for a variety of purposes short of a revolutionary seizure of power, such as coercion or intimidation, vengeance or punishment. Revolutionary terrorism brings about political revolution, i.e. a fundamental change in the power structure and often, in addition, fundamental changes in the socio-economic order.

The aim of any revolution is to achieve tactical objectives:

1. It is a group phenomenon with a leadership and an ideology, and can develop alternative institutional structures.

2. The organisation of violence and terrorism is done by specialist conspiratorial and paramilitary organs within the revolutionary movement.

3. Terrorism can be employed as can urban guerrilla warfare to convert the political crisis into armed struggle by the people against the military powers.

4. Both the political terrorist and urban guerrilla try to 'militarise' the political struggle and to get the people to blame the government for their discontents and to turn against the regime.

5. For the fanatical revolutionary, terrorism becomes a cover for their revolutionary virtue and a theatre of revolutionary deeds that can be glamorised and romanticised to help the weak believe they are strong and that the revolution is on the way.

Terrorism can become an addiction to murder in the name of liberation and justice which in reality is an urge to rebel.

6. Revolutionaries are enthusiastic but at the same time incompetent, in the context that the desire to be a guerrilla has, at times, divorced the rebel from reality and led that person to pursue a dream into a fantasy.

In the twentieth century the major thrust of contemporary revolutionary activity has been towards guerrilla strategy, urban or rural, focused narrowly on the target regime, rather than on the international system or distant secondary opponents. Despite allegations of revolutionary incompetence, there has been a growing indication of worldwide cooperation among revolutionary groups.

Unconventional warfare

Unconventional warfare is an act, process or instance of waging war, conflict, struggle or strife, which does not conform to accepted rules or standards. Some degree of popular support and collaboration is a priceless asset to the wagers of such wars.

The decisive war against terrorism has to be waged in the realm of intelligence and counter-intelligence. The more the security forces pursue the political and domestic goals of the population, the more likely the counter-insurgency would succeed. Insurgencies or counter-revolutionaries need support from the population and, to be successful, counter-insurgencies must remove that support.

Civil war

Civil war is a war between parties, factions or inhabitants of different regions within the same nation.

Civil war undermines stability and in a pluralist society, i.e. one with groups having distinctive ethnic origins, cultural forms and religions, the bulwarks of stability can be slender. Security intelligence and the rule of law are maintained by the police and army, the intelligence services and the judiciary. If these become weak or corrupt, the rising tide of drug abuse, crime, political violence, public disorder and civil war can all too easily sweep the bulwarks away, leading to an authoritarian government of the right, dominated by the army or the left, the latter usually a professionally organised revolutionary party.

Colonial wars

Many such wars have been associated with terrorism and have been lengthy and costly. Fighters against the former colonial powers argued that colonialism was violence in its natural state and would only yield when confronted with greater violence. Legitimate targets included colonial administrators, high-ranking security forces officers and business personnel supporting the regime.

Terrorism in colonial struggles emerged post-1945. Colonialism began to be viewed as a relic of a bygone era by many citizens of the colonial powers and, indeed, by non-colonial governments. Public opinion across the globe inhibited the colonial powers from displaying the military might they were capable of, and which in the past they would have employed to put down the insurrection.

It is doubtful that anti-colonial guerrillas fully understood the result of their actions but the link they forged between violent action and an audience succeeded in effectively neutralising the military muscle of the colonial powers. Their acts of violence were able to achieve domestic and international political pressure on the colonial government in excess of the pressure they could have exerted militarily.

Religious conflicts

Many terrorist groups are characterised by a strong religious element. There have been anti-colonial rationalist movements such as the Jewish terrorist organisations active in pre-independence Israel, the Catholic IRA, the Protestant loyalists groups such as the Red Hand Commandos and the Palestine Liberation

Organisation. More extreme religious groups have surfaced in Iran and Afghanistan, and the Islamic Hamas terrorists have been responsible for a wave of suicide attacks in Israel over the past decade, and especially since September 2001.

The connection between religion and terrorism is not new. More than 2,000 years ago the first acts of what we now call terrorism were perpetrated by:

▶ **Zealots** – the word zealot means an immoderate partisan or a fanatical enthusiast – were religious fanatics such as the Jewish Zealots who fought from AD 66 to AD 73 against the Roman Empire's occupation of what is now Israel.

▶ **Thugs** – the word thug ('vicious or brutal ruffians') is derived from a seventh-century religious cult that terrorised India until its suppression in the mid-nineteenth century.

▶ **Assassins** – those who undertake to put another to death by treacherous violence – was the name of a radical offshoot of the Islamic Shia Ismaili sect who between AD 1090 and 1272 fought to repel the Christian crusaders attempting to conquer present-day Syria and Iran.

The Iranian revolution in 1979 witnessed the re-emergence of modern religious terrorism and soon none of the world's major religions could claim to be immune to the same volatile mixture of faith, fanaticism and violence.

The prominence of religion as the major driving force behind international terrorism in the 1990s was proven by the fact that the most serious attacks of the decade have had a salient religious purpose and dimension:

▶ the nerve gas attack in 1995 on the Tokyo subway system perpetrated by an apocalyptic Japanese religious cult: 12 died and over 3,500 were injured

▶ the bombing in 1995 of the Oklahoma City Federal office by Christian Patriots seeking to foment a nationwide revolution: 168 died

- ▶ the gun and hand-grenade attack carried out by Egyptian Islamic militants on a group of Western tourists outside their Cairo hotel in 1996: 18 killed

- ▶ the bloodletting by Islamic extremists in Algeria: claimed the lives of an estimated 75,000 persons since 1992.

To a religious terrorist, violence is a duty from on high, executed in direct response to some theological imperative. Religion is conveyed by sacred test imparted via clerical authorities claiming to speak for the divine and serving as a legitimising force. Ultimately, they wish to seek fundamental changes to the existing order. Their ideology and intentions are politically radical and personally fanatical. Such groups are mercurial and unpredictable, especially at the dawn of the third millennium.

Ethnic conflict

Situations in which ethnic divisions coexist with conflict over what constitutes the legitimate territorial boundaries of political authority are capable of generating violence, as in Northern Ireland.

Ethnic nationalism is a complex issue. Ethnic factors can be organised and rendered meaningful in various ways, thus becoming elements of any number of identities. It often deserves its reputation in part precisely because it is not easy to define.

- ▶ An ethnic conflict may arise out of these discordant definitions, e.g. Croats, Serbs and Bosnians can all be described as South Slavs, or are they members of different ethnicities?

- ▶ The predominance of one ethnic group in a state can create dangers for, and provoke a revolt by, other ethnic groups, e.g. the Tamils in Sri Lanka, the Hutus in Rwanda, the Ibos in Nigeria.

- ▶ There is also the risk of external intervention justified on the grounds of ethnic solidarity Serbia to protect Serbs in

Croatia, Armenia to protect Armenians in Ngorno Karabakh.

A world in which the borders of ethnic groups are those of nation-states is both inconceivable given the confusion about what is ethnic and the pattern of ethnic groups and also a recipe for permanent conflict in so far as an emphasis on this single factor magnifies the differences among peoples. When ethnic national-ism turns into a doctrine of racial superiority, catastrophic effects can ensue, e.g. Hitler's attacks on the Jews and the ethnic cleansing resulting from the break-up of the former Yugoslavia.

In the Cold War era, 1945–90, the potential conflicts were ideological. In the New World Order of the 1990s the potential and actual conflict has been ethnic. In the fragile arena of international politics there is a heterogeneous collection of new states produced by the collapse of the Soviet Union.

The principle of self-determination appears mainly as a factor of fragmentation and turbulence more than as a lever of human liberation. It is a threat to the territorial integrity of states with secessions and splits both actual (Ukraine, Central Asia, Georgia, Azerbaijan, Eritrea) or potential (Sri Lanka, Quebec). Moreover, it often clashes with another area of contemporary international law: respect for and protection of human rights individually or, in the case of minorities, collectively. The Yugoslav tragedy provides many examples.

The dimensions of ethnic and sub-ethnic conflict
When empires break up, such conflicts are widespread, as in the case of the Soviet Union and within some of the units that resulted from its disintegration (in Russia the wars in Chechnya, Georgia and Azerbaijan). We can also see this when the state structure is weak (e.g. in Yugoslavia after Tito, Sudan, Rwanda) or weakened by war (e.g. in Iraq in 1991, Afghanistan). Repression may be ruthless enough to provoke collective resistance but not enough to wipe it out (e.g. the Kurds in Turkey and Iraq) or a minority may receive support from an outside power dominated by the same ethnic group (e.g. the Turks in Cyprus, the Albanians in Kosovo and pan-Tutsism in central and eastern Africa).

Ethnic and sub-ethnic conflict can disrupt international relations and domestic affairs by destroying the status quo. It puts into jeopardy existing orders, as occurred with the rebellions in Nigeria. It produces huge masses of refugees which can provoke violence or hostile and inhumane reactions in the affected countries; it fuels lasting conflicts among states, such as those between India and Pakistan, Greece and Turkey, Israel and Syria, Israel and the potential Palestinian state.

Ethnic conflict can be intractable and murderous. Warlords come and go, gang members can melt away into the country and ideological armies fade or reach a compromise, but ethnic and religious feelings (as in Northern Ireland) have a way of surviving, even if they go underground for a period of time Ultimately genocide can result from ethnic/religious intolerance.

Minorities

Minorities can be an issue on which terrorism thrives. Terrorists argue they are the minority's protectors. A sensitive region like the former Yugoslavia proves how revolutionaries can be tempted by the ethnic mix:

▶ Vojvodina – the potential conflict between Hungary and Serbia has been a threat over the Hungarian minority: 55% Serb, 19% Hungarian and 5% Croat

▶ Slovenia – declared independence in 1991: 90% Slovene

▶ Croatia – declared independence in 1991 but engaged in civil war with Serbia over Serb minority in east and southeast: 70% Croat and 14% Serb

▶ Bosnia and Hercegovina – territory claimed by both Serbia and Croatia: 39% Muslims, 31% Serb and 18% Croat

▶ Kosovo – suppression by Serbia led to civil war, 1998–99, and NATO intervention to free the land: 91% Albanian and 8% Serb

▶ Macedonia – declared independence in 1991, but the territory was disputed by Serbia, Bulgaria and Greece: 67% Macedonian, 20% or more Albanian.

Yugoslavia has seen examples of:

▶ *irredentism* – the doctrine of 'redeeming' territory from foreign rule (reincorporating into one's country territory formerly belonging to it)

▶ *regionalism* – the desire for economic autonomy for a region

▶ *separatism* – the desire for a separate country for an ethnic group on political grounds.

Guerrilla warfare

Guerrillas fight 'little wars' as part of an indigenous fighting unit against regular armed forces. Their targets are the military and other security forces of the opponent, not the non-combatants. They are predominantly fighting counterforces. Guerrillas are direct indigenous representatives of the reference group and fight on their native soil – they generally enjoy the tacit support of major sections of the population.

Guerrilla wars have been fought throughout history by small peoples against invading or occupying armies, by regular soldiers operating in the enemy's rear, by peasants rising against big landowners, by bandits both 'social' and 'asocial'. Uniquely in Latin America guerrilla warfare continued to be the prevailing form of military conflict in the absence of strong regular armies.

Guerrilla warfare is decisive only when the anti-guerrilla side is prevented for military or political reasons from committing its full resources to the struggle. Guerrilla movements need bases and they cannot operate without a steady flow of supplies. This type of warfare often occurs in areas in which such wars have occurred before. There is negative correlation between guerrilla warfare and the degree of economic development.

Types of guerrilla warfare
During the nineteenth and twentieth centuries there have been three main types of guerrilla war:

1. Wars directed against foreign occupants, either in the framework of a general war or after the defeat of the regular army, and against colonial rule.

2. Such warfare has been the favourite tactic of separatist minority movements fighting central governments, for example the Basques and the Kurds.

3. Wars against native incumbents have been the rule in Latin America and in a few other countries such as Burma (Myanmar). However, the national patriotic element has always been heavily emphasised even if domestic rulers were the target; they were attacked as foreign mercenaries by the true patriots fighting for national unity or independence.

Traditionally peasants have constituted the most important mass basis of guerrilla movements.

Reasons for joining guerrilla bands
People have joined guerrilla bands for a variety of reasons:

▶ patriotism

▶ occupation of the homeland by foreigners

▶ resentment directed against the colonial power

▶ personal grievances – humiliation, material deprivation, brutalities committed by the occupying forces

▶ to fight domestic contenders – guerrillas stress political or social grievances such as the struggle against tyranny, unequal distribution of income, government inefficiency, corruption and 'betrayal' and the unpopularity of the ruling group.

▶ as an outlet for personal aggression – guerrilla warfare provides opportunities for settling accounts with one's enemies and conveys power to those hitherto powerless.

Sophistication of guerrilla warfare
Organisation, propaganda and terror have always been essential

parts of guerrilla warfare but their importance has increased over recent years and have become more sophisticated:

▶ Organisation implies the existence of a political party or movement providing assistance such as money and intelligence.

▶ Propaganda is important in civil wars when the majority of the population takes a neutral, passive attitude in the struggle between incumbents and insurgents.

▶ Terror is used as a deliberate strategy to demoralise the government by disrupting its control. It seeks to demonstrate one's own strength and to frighten collaborators.

Basically guerrilla war is the struggle for the support of the majority of the people.

Guevara's theory of revolution

Che Guevara was a Latin American revolutionary and guerrilla, a fighter of Argentinian origin and Fidel Castro's right-hand man in the Cuban revolution of 1959. In the 1960s he went to South America to spread his revolutionary message and was killed by the Bolivian army in 1967. Since his death 'Che' as Guevara is affectionately known, became the legendary hero of a cult among left-wing students and other young radicals in the Western world. Guevara's ideas on revolutionary and guerrilla warfare became the basis of discussions about the overall strategy of revolutionary activity and the importance of the guerrilla in a strategy of insurrection.

The key issues
1. People's forces win a war against a regular army.

2. One should wait until all the conditions are favourable for a revolution, for example an insurrection.

3. There is an armed struggle in the countryside.

4. Options in the armed struggle are:

– an insurrectionary rising;
– a rural guerrilla campaign;
– an urban guerrilla campaign.

Weaknesses in Guevara's thought
1. Too much responsibility is assumed.

2. The inherent nature of conspiracy hinders internal communication.

3. Incomprehension rises, disagreement hardens and ultimately scepticism sets in.

The Marighela model on the course of guerrilla warfare

Carlos Marighela was a Brazilian revolutionary whose mini-manual for the urban guerrilla became the basis for urban guerrilla activity in the 1980s and 1990s. There were four stages:

▶ *Stage 1*. Marighela called for the immediate inception of guerrilla activity with organisations growing through unleashing revolutionary action and calling for extreme violence. From this there would be two forces: (a) urban guerrilla warfare (proletariat and students), with the aims being expropriation of attacking government forces and attacking US finance/capitalism; and (b) psychological warfare involving students and low-level terrorism involving propaganda.

▶ *Stage 2*. A government would be provoked into repression (a political situation therefore would become a military situation) and there would be polarisation of social groups. Mobile rural guerrilla groups would emerge.

▶ *Stage 3*. A people's army would result which would inflict defeats on government forces followed by a general strike.

▶ *Stage 4*. A seizure of power would occur. A crisis point for guerrillas would be reached when activities reached a scale requiring central coordination.

The Debray model of guerrilla warfare

This model was developed by Regis Debray, a French revolutionary theorist involved in the urban and rural guerrilla activity in South America in the 1960s. He argued that foreign career revolutionaries and selected indigenous participants would come together as a guerrilla force. Three phases would then develop:

1. With maximum secrecy, jungle/mountain reconnaissance would take place to allow guerrillas to adapt to the environment. A small training operation would occur against the regime. Operational columns would be formed.

2. Guerrilla bases would be established and there would be an increase in numbers. Regional guerrillas and urban squads would be set up.

3. The resultant people's army would then go on the defensive. Regional urban groups would keep government forces tied down, mobile forces would attack selected targets and there would be a general strike coinciding with a conventional offensive on the capital.

Primarily Debray believed that intellectuals were invaluable to the success of any revolutionary cause but that when they took part in such activity they had a bad conscience. The struggle against oppression was his overriding concern approaching the status of a fight for a sacred cause.

The conflict spectrum

The conflict spectrum features in many aspects of the analysis of revolutionary conflict.

▶ *Terrorism* – indiscriminate acts of political violence and attacks on 'soft' targets (civilian or military). These activities can be criminal acts or like those perpetrated by the Popular Front for the Liberation of Palestine (PFLP), the Irish Republican Army (IRA), the Red Army Faction (RAF) or the Basque separatist organisation Euzkadi Ta Azkatasuna (ETA).

► *Counter-terrorism* – basically involves special tactics, such as used by Delta Force in USA and the GSG9 in Germany, or private militias and vigilante groups.

► *Low intensity conflict* – is a form of revolution and counter-revolution and can include wars of natural liberation, civil war, and ethnic and religious turmoil. Nicaragua in the 1980s is a classic example.

► *Conventional warfare* – includes major land wars such as that between Iran and Iraq and the Soviets in Afghanistan.

► *Nuclear warfare* – is a first strike an option? Or total destruction?

Conditions conducive to urban violence

► Self-conscious segregation of ethnic, cultural or religious minority.

► Economic deprivation and political oppression linked to unemployment and inflation.

► External encouragement may be provided by Communists.

► There is a historic 'them' to blame – churches, whites, capitalists.

► Frustrated elites can be especially dangerous as they can manipulate violent power.

Tutorial

Progress questions

1. How can revolutionary conflict exhibit fear?

2. What are the differences between revolution and terrorism?

3. Are not all wars in some ways unconventional?

4. Religion and terrorism can often produce fanaticism. Why?

5.   Provide some reasons for the mixed success of guerrilla fighters.

6.   Is the conflict spectrum too broad for nations to control?

Discussion points

1.   Is it a pointless exercise to differentiate between terrorists and guerrillas?

2.   Can a differentiation be made between unconventional warfare and revolutionary conflict?

3.   Are civil wars an inevitable consequence of colonial wars?

Practical assignments

1.   Provide a detailed analysis of which factors you deem most important in providing a model for guerrilla warfare.

2.   Provide a workable definition of revolutionary conflict.

3.   How do you distinguish between terrorism and guerrilla warfare?

2

The Problems of Definition

One-minute summary – In this chapter we will discuss the problems of defining the terms 'guerrilla' and 'terrorist'. In particular we will explore:

▶ pathological, political and economic perspectives
▶ definitional problems
▶ definitional variables
▶ characteristics differentiating guerrillas from terrorists.

The problems of definition

A definition is basically an equation: it says what a word is meant to mean. However, with regard to the concept of terrorism, the emotive nature of the subject matter, the threat inherent in the term and the political discourse all make its definition a complex matter.

Key participants

It is broadly accepted that there are at least five major participants in the process of terror:

▶ the persons behind the violence

▶ the victims at the time of the incident

▶ the wider target group in a society over which terrorists claim power or terror

▶ observers of the terror

▶ international public opinion, often gleaned from the media.

Key elements

But these are mere skeletal issues – it is the flesh and muscle of the
argument which hold the attention of governments.

▶ There is hardly a definition which does not contain the word
violence. However, rather than being considered as a
technique of applying violence which in principle can be
used by anyone in all sorts of conflict situations, the concept
is linked only to certain actions only for certain types of
conflict. Often the hackneyed phrase 'one man's terrorist is
another man's patriot' is used, proving that the concept has
been subjected to a double standard, and an 'in-group, out-
group' distinction.

▶ Some governments are prone to label as terrorism all violent
acts committed by their political opponents while anti-
government extremists claim to be the victims of government
terror.

▶ Political sociologists argue that no definition can be reached
because the very process of definition is in itself part of the
wider complexities of ideology or political objectives.
Definitions support the argument that the perspectives
change according to when and where the terrorist act takes
place.

▶ The question of the definition of terrorism is central to an
understanding of the phenomenon and to the success of any
rational measures directed against it. To many observers
almost any act of violence may be included under the rubric
of terrorism.

▶ Some observers do not see terrorism as violent acts carried
out within a revolutionary context which a number of people
would recognise as terrorist.

▶ Confusion can arise over the similarity of behaviour observed
when a violent act is carried out by a politically motivated
individual, a criminal or the mentally unbalanced.

▶ Terrorism is a moral issue and attempts at definition are
predicated on the assumption that some cases of political

violence are justifiable whereas others are not. One of the problems of implementing criminal sanctions occurs in the case of acts of terrorism that produce a terror outcome by threats of violence, without actual physical injury to any human or non-human targets.

▶ The word terrorism is often used with qualifying terms – 'often', 'mainly', 'generally' and 'usually'. These qualifiers allow for the injection of personal views in deciding whether a particular act is or is not 'terrorist'. Conversely defining terrorism by focusing on the nature of the act rather than on the identity of the perpetrators or the nature of their cause makes a substantial degree of objectivity possible.

▶ Although specially constituted United Nations committees have continually condemned acts of international terrorism in principle, they have exempted from their definition of such acts those activities which derive from the inalienable right to self-determination and independence of all peoples under colonial and racist regimes, and in particular the struggles of national liberation movements. It is argued that this is in accordance with the purposes and principles of the Charter and the relevant resolutions of the organs of the United Nations.

▶ By definition terrorism is an act that seeks to influence a population significantly larger than the immediate target. The quality of the public's understanding and its response to terrorism of all varieties is highly significant.

▶ Many of the definitional problems can be found in the scientific and ideological discourse on violence. Terrorism has been defined in terms of violation – violation of the corporal integrity of the state, violation of territorial or special integrity, violation of moral and legal decency, violation of rules and expectations and even as violation of self-esteem, dignity and autonomy. A definitional struggle has thus arisen between those who claim an exception at law for certain manifestly harmful forms of conduct and those who will not admit it.

▶ Definitional approaches which relate merely to acts of violence, the threat or use of violence, repressive acts, and similar categorisations are incomplete and unhelpful in terms of meaning and effective guidance for decision-making. These types of approach ignore the critical need for a focus upon the use of intense fear or anxiety to coerce a primary target into behaviour or attitudinal patterns sought in connection with a demanded power outcome.

▶ Terrorism's success is measured not only by its ability to topple the social order but also by its ability to loosen that order in symbolic terms by weakening the law-making opportunities of elected officials and casting doubt on the concept of rights in society and the obligations of the state. Vague generalised definitions can mean that the scope of the analysis is too broad and so the findings may be meaningless. Too narrow a definition means there is little opportunity for comparative analysis which may reveal patterns common to various acts of terrorism.

▶ Definitions of terrorism have to be studied within the overall subject matter of terrorism and related to its history, philosophy, psychology, sociology, politics, statistics, language and law. In the field of terrorism there is no agreement about any single definition, but there is considerable agreement about the elements which definitions should contain. Open-mindedness and objectivity can be of some help in the problem of definition.

Definitional variables regarding terrorism

Points to consider in a definition of terrorism include:

▶ unconditional warfare – terrorist campaigns

▶ is all politically motivated crime terrorism?

▶ incidents designed to create terror

▶ terrorism as the weapon of minorities

▶ differing perception of events: terrorist or freedom fighter?

▶ definitional issues under international law: these can be a collection of different definitions proposed by various national governments.

As a result of studying the tactics and strategy of terrorism we can now attempt to define terrorism as an organised system of extreme and violent intimidation to create instability within democracies. International terrorists seek to launch indiscriminate and unpredictable attacks on groups (police, army, multinationals or nations) to change the politico-economic balance of the world.

Pathological, political and economic perspectives

Terrorism can be viewed from contrasting pathological, political and economic perspectives:

1. *Pathological view* – terrorism can lead to revenge against society and destruction of the establishment. Pathological behaviour of a tyrannical government can be caused by excessive fear.

2. *Political view* – terrorism contains components of the ideological socio-psychological and military-strategic. Terror can be used by individuals and groups against the state to seize control in order to clear the way for takeover by the new regime and to punish and destroy those in authority. It can equally be used by the state authorities to control cities, and punish and/or destroy potential and actual 'enemies'.

3. *Economic view* – terrorism can be seen in terms of domestic, organised crime. The state can enforce and make possible economic exploitation of the population by state authorities through submission.

Differentiating between terrorists and guerrillas

Terrorists

Terrorists have certain characteristics:

▶ an urban focus

▶ the object of attack is property, civilians, military and government officials

▶ terrorists operate in small bands (from 3 to 20 members)

▶ they instigate a challenge to specific policies and laws

▶ there is either a limited or no attempt to control territory or to function as the government of record, e.g to collect taxes, 'legislate' and enforce laws

▶ primarily terrorism is a form of psychological warfare tied to criminal violence and the threat of violence.

Guerrillas

On the other hand, guerrillas generally have:

▶ a rural focus

▶ as an object of their attack, the property or persons of the military, police and government

▶ an organisation which can grow quite large and eventually take the form of a conventional military force

▶ the ability to challenge the very legitimacy of the nation state

▶ the power to establish a parallel government and all that it implies, such as laws, police functions and corrections

▶ the ability to be perceived as being able to create criminal violence allied to threats and other psychological strategies.

Tutorial

Progress questions

1. Discuss whether problems over agreeing a definition are good reasons for government inaction?

2. Describe how one could measure the success of terrorism.

Discussion points

1. How far should one become involved in the semantics of terrorism?

2. Do terrorists and revolutionaries really conform to any definition?

3. Are the definitional variables too wide-ranging?

4. Pathological, economic, political – which aspect of terrorism do you consider is the most lethal?

Practical assignments

1. Try to draft a workable definition of terrorism which could be legally binding and effective.

2. Summarise the problems you consider worthy of analysis in coming to a consensus on definition.

3. Consider what further terrorist motivations could be added to the pathological, political and economic factors.

3

Conditions of State Terrorism and Conflict Resolution

One-minute summary – In this chapter we will discuss the conditions of state terrorism and conflict resolution and the challenges facing society. In particular we will explore:

▶ the state and political ideology
▶ social heterogeneity and inequality in the global environment
▶ conflict resolution, obstacles and handicaps
▶ the vicious circle of terrorism
▶ democratisation and terrorism
▶ myths of terrorism
▶ dissident terrorism.

Conditions of state terrorism

Development of conditions initially set by the challengers

The greater the political threat posed by challenges, the greater the likelihood that the regime will respond with violence. The greater the latent support for revolutionary challengers in a population, the greater the likelihood that a regime will respond with terrorism.

Challengers who rely on terrorist and guerrilla tactics are likely to be countered by state terror. Regimes are more likely to use terrorism against politically marginal groups than opposition groups that have no influence on, or supporters among, the elite.

The state and political ideology

Weak regimes are more likely to use violence in response to

challengers than strong regimes. Elites who have secured and maintained their positions by violent means are likely to choose violent responses to future challenges.

Successful situational uses of state terror in polarised societies are likely to lead to institutionalised terror and to the pre-emptive use of terror to maintain political control. The initial decision of a challenged elite to use state terror is usually modelled on the successful uses of state terror by others. Democratic principles and institutions inhibit political elites from using state violence in general and terror specifically.

Social heterogeneity and inequality

The greater the heterogeneity and stratification in a society, the greater the likelihood that a regime will use violence as a principle means of social control. Minority elites in highly stratified societies are likely to use terror routinely as an instrument of rule.

The global environment

Regimes facing external threats are likely to use violence against domestic opponents. Regimes involved in proxy big power conflicts are likely to use the most extreme forms of violence against challengers, including state terrorism. Peripheral status in the world system increases the likelihood that regimes that rule by violence can do so with impunity.

Conflict resolution – obstacles and handicaps

A policy of world order requires that the many sources of global or regional turbulence be dealt with in ways that would minimise violent conflict among states, reduce injustice among and within states and prevent dangerous violations of rights within them. The obstacles are formidable.

The model of world order

The model of world order that underlies the League of Nations and the United Nations is unworkable as it is based on the notion of collective security. International society has neither the centralised government, judicial system or police that characterise a well-ordered state, nor a consensus on what constitutes a crime that exists in domestic affairs.

Coercion
Coercion seldom works as an instrument of order in world affairs:

▶ It often punishes the innocent even more than the guilty, such as the hapless civilians.

▶ Conflicts have to be resolved by negotiation

▶ Weapons at the disposal of the parties stifle negotiation.

Domestic disorder
Internal disorder or repression can create international conflict, particularly when a government violently attacks a large part of its own population, whether this corresponds to the legal definition of genocide or not.

Human rights
Grave violations of fundamental human rights by oppressive regimes can cause instability.

Weapons of mass destruction
There may be a clandestine build-up of weapons of mass destruction, especially in states with deep unsettled grievances towards neighbours.

Peacekeeping organisations
Many existing organisations for peacekeeping and enforcement are inadequately equipped for conflict resolution, their resources are too small, their staff too politically constructed, their procedures too clumsy, their agendas overburdened, their legitimacy too contested. In the UN, the General Assembly is unwieldy and the Security Council is frozen by the obsolete definitions of the great powers deriving from the Second World War.

International and regional organisations
International and regional organisations cannot be effective unless a powerful state or group of states is willing to take responsibility for exerting pressure or taking action.

Financial support

World leadership also requires money: one can't have order on the cheap. Consider the cost of rehabilitating Eastern Europe, of preventing convulsions in the former Soviet Union, narrowing the gap between rich and poor countries to prevent famine and huge population flows. Consider also the cost of providing debt relief to many of the bankrupt countries, of protecting the environment and of compensating domestic arms manufacturers deprived of external outlets. Any attempt to solve such intractable problems requires cash, but unless these varied issues – and many more – are resolved, the seeds of revolutionary conflict will grow.

Position of the US

The ambivalence of the United States can be a problem. If the country chooses to concentrate on its own domestic issues, there will be little money and attention available for involvement in the wider world.

The vicious circle of terrorism

Terrorists define their own form of terrorism a number of ways:

1. Revolutionary terror can be organisational. Terror in the form of an allegiance can relate to violence and mass support, and functional terror means that strategic advantage can be gained through specific action. Provocative terror can also be appealing as this includes exploitation and escalation, and in its symbiotic form, terror can link the victim as a figure who represents the epitome of the enemy.

2. The actual desire to achieve destruction can be the motivation for the act. The perpetrator of such destructive behaviour also enjoys taking hostages and seeing them suffer.

3. The vicious circle is the perpetrators of violence, the victims concerned and the role of the security units in trying to prevent more terrorism.

Democratisation and terrorism

New democratic regimes could not and did not rid their countries of long-standing terrorism and insurgencies. Terrorists and revolutionaries form a concrete political force against democracy. Some countries respond to terrorism and violence in drastic ways. Consider the military takeovers in Turkey, South Korea and Pakistan in recent decades.

Latin America

In Latin America there was neither reform nor revolution, but instead repression in the form of military and bureaucratic authoritarian regimes. In some countries on the continent, political party leaders had a stake in employing the methods in which they were skilled – negotiation, compromise and elections – and in avoiding the tactics of terrorism and insurgency in which others would excel.

In South America, much debate occurred within opposition groups as to the merits of different types of target and the morality and effectiveness of random terrorist attacks against civilians. Opposition groups committed to violence also debated the relative merits of rural and urban guerrilla warfare and the desirability and timing of major offensives and popular uprisings.

Myths of state terrorism

When victimised by a terrorist outrage, many people, including political leaders, understandably want to strike back, to inflict a painful retribution on those responsible. Such an emotional reaction provides a powerful, though not always rational, under-pinning to one myth about how best to deal with terrorism. Severe retribution in extreme form pictures those resorting to terrorism as 'mad dogs' and death is the only cure for the threat posed by a mad dog.

▶ *The myth of conciliation* sees the capacity of conciliation to cure terrorism rather than emphasising the ruthless character of the perpetrators of terrorism and the cynical manipulations of their sponsors. This myth stresses the origins of frustration felt by those who feel driven to resort to terrorism. By taking account of the conditions that nurture extremist politics, this myth encourages a counter-terrorist policy aimed at alleviating the root causes of radical discontent. The role of external sponsors has been played down, just as the opposing myth stresses the significance of such support.

▶ *The myth of social disconnection* sees dissident terrorism as largely rooted in a crisis of 'social disconnection' existing between militant intellectuals and the masses they wish to lead. Terrorism in this context is seen as an intellectual attempting to shoot his way out of isolation. Not many governments are enthusiastic about policies providing political therapy to alienated intellectuals, nor are they able to make concessions that would satisfy radical demands.

▶ *The myth of retribution* stresses immediate response at the expense of long-term solutions.

▶ *The myth of social cure*, by focusing on the presumed underlying causes, fails to address immediate security concerns.

▶ *The myth of knowing the terrorist* as a cure for all evil is advice more easily offered than followed.

Responding to dissident terrorism

Factors shaping our response

The ideological aims of the dissident groups
Groups desiring the destruction of the established order and/or its radical transformation would not be open to much compromise of their political objectives. Greater autonomy offers greater promise for negotiated settlement.

The relative isolation/representativeness of the dissident group
Punitive attacks against unpopular groups might be more

successful than those against groups supported by a large section of the population.

Role of terrorism in dissident strategy
As such groups become more representative and successfully organise their communities for resistance, the role of terrorist tactics may diminish. Any state which sees rebellion as only committed by an isolated band of criminal terrorists is in for a shock.

External sponsors
The more autonomous the dissident movement, the less effective will be the counter-terrorist policies which concentrate on external conspiracy theories. External sponsorship and conspiracy comprise an element of global terrorism and the variation of sponsorship makes it impossible to substitute facile consistency for serious analysis. Counter-terrorist measures which adopt a quick-fix solution are bound to fail.

Tutorial

Progress questions
1. Which conditions of state terrorism are the most difficult to control?

2. Analyse the reasons behind the global environment causing terrorism.

3. Is conflict resolution more of a possibility legally than practically? Discuss.

4. Show ways in which criminality can lead to terrorism.

5. Define a myth in relation to violence – is it a feasible proposition?

Discussion points
1. Is discussion of democratisation and terrorism a contradiction?

2. How have many of the myths about terrorism developed?

Practical assignments

1. Produce your own set of conditions of state terrorism.

2. Analyse how the vicious circle of terrorism can be broken.

3. Suggest a set of basic principles to overcome the obstacles and handicaps to conflict resolution.

4

The Role of the Media

One-minute summary – In this chapter we will discuss the critical role of the media in revolutionary warfare. In particular we will explore:

▶ the media and public opinion
▶ the contagion effect of media coverage
▶ terrorism as a form of communication
▶ the media and the authorities – scope and limits of cooperation
▶ censorship and terrorism – pros and cons
▶ propaganda issues posed by terrorists.

The media and public opinion

A free media needs a free press, but terrorism needs a propaganda platform. So in all Western countries, the news media faces a dilemma. Is it possible to keep citizens informed of daily events, including the often graphic tragedy of terrorism, without becoming to some degree propagandists for the perpetrators?

News or propaganda?
The question of whether information is news or propaganda is very important. Even basic news stories about terrorism can involve agonising decisions.

1. Do such news stories contribute to the free marketplace of ideas helping people to understand the central issues of their day? Or do they give terrorists a megaphone through which to spread their message of fear to their ultimate target – the public at large?

2. Do the news media provide the oxygen of publicity on which terrorism thrives, and thereby help in the spread of sedition?

3. Does extensive coverage by the media turn the terrorists into folk heroes, or does such coverage produce a sense of outrage – public revulsion against terrorist acts and demands for tougher measures by the government?

4. Does journalism put so much pressure on the government that it acts irresponsibly or does it provide important information to officials, since in hostile situations reporters can sometimes go where decision-makers in government dare not venture?

Many people and organisations consider the media to be hooked on terrorism. To some people in the media, terrorism is drama. In efforts to captivate viewers do the media cover terrorist incidents whenever possible? Or do they (as they themselves believe) just report the facts simply and fairly?

International terrorism derives credibility from the extensive news coverage which such acts attract. In such a situation journalists seem to fear manipulation by terrorists as much as they do government control. Tensions run high in terrorist situations, especially when the event is ongoing or when hostages are involved. Television and newspaper reporters usually arrive at the scene of a terrorist incident within minutes of the security forces. Distrust and distaste often dominate their interactions from the start.

However, coverage of terrorism is not helpful to terrorist groups. Terrorists want to use the media for propaganda purposes, but the media focus on violence. News reports rarely explain the causes of the terrorism and they almost never portray terrorism in a favourable light. The reason is clear – far from being a tool for terrorism, the media serve the interests of the government.

The contagion effect of media coverage

▶ Media reports promote fear and magnify the threat in the public mind. That fear spreads.

▶ The media also influence the way terrorists select their targets to spread violence – terrorists select targets for maximum publicity.

▶ The media have become the vehicle for the psychological impact of terrorism.

Terrorism as a form of communication

Rapid communications allow reporters to travel to the war zone and bring the battlefield to the general public. Public opinion has become a major aspect of modern warfare and mobilising public opinion is deemed a necessary strategy to achieve victory. This attitude is reflected in terrorism.

The media have been able to exploit terrorists for their own needs. It is hard to define terrorism but the media have done so by applying labels to terrorist actions. The media are selective about calling violent events terrorism, but when they do the public is provided with a *de facto* definition. The media label terrorism and cover it according to their own needs.

However, terrorists learn their tactics and copy methods from the mass media. Media coverage serves as a motivation for terrorism.

Violence seems to increase during media coverage and therefore the mass media have become the perfect instrument of violent communication.

The media and the authorities

The scope and limits of cooperation
The authorities can assume full control of the dissemination of information and news through the media. To some extent control can be taken by the authorities through the issuing of authoritative statements. The authorities can release a limited number of authoritative communiqués for the normal newsreels. Cooperation can be established between the authorities and one or a few electronic public mass media.

Censorship and terrorism

The issue of censorship is one on which most analysts agree. Few seem to advocate direct censorship, but a variety of lesser degrees of media control are frequently advocated. It may be possible to invoke some of these without violating individual rights and the freedoms of speech and press. Internal methods of self-regulation are the most frequently recommended means of dealing with the press.

Opinion in democratic societies is very much polarised on this issue.

Arguments for censorship

1. Insurgent terrorists use the media as a platform for political propaganda which also helps them to recruit new members to their movement.

2. Since publicity is a major and in some cases the unique reward sought by terrorists, censorship would make terrorism a less desirable strategy.

3. Detailed coverage of incidents by the media provides potential terrorists with a model that increases their chances of success in their own acts.

4. Information broadcast during incidents can be useful to terrorists.

5. Media presence during acts of hostage-taking can endanger hostages.

6. Reporting on acts of terrorism can produce imitative acts.

7. In cases of kidnapping, media reports can cause panic with the kidnapper so that he kills the victim.

8. People who have so little respect for other people's lives as terrorists do should not be enabled to command public attention simply because they use violence.

9. Sadistic behaviour among the public might be encouraged by the reporting of terrorist acts.

10. Media reports on terrorist outrages might lead to vigilantism and uncontrolled revenge acts against the group the terrorists claim to speak for.

11. Negative news demoralises the public while 'good' news makes us feel good.

Arguments against censorship

1. If the media were to keep quiet about terrorist atrocities the perpetrators of violence might be judged less negatively by sections of the public.

2. With psychotic terrorists, publicity can be a substitute for violence. Without media attention their threats might be translated into acts.

3. Political terrorists boycotted by the media might step up their level of violence until the media *have* to cover their deeds.

4. If the media did not report on terrorism rumours would spread, which might be worse than the worst media reporting.

5. During siege situations, the media presence can prevent the police from engaging in indefensible tactics which cause unnecessary loss of lives among hostages and terrorists.

6. If terrorism were to be treated with silence, governments could label all sorts of quasi or non-terrorist activities by political dissenters as terrorism. Uncontrolled government actions might be the result.

7. If the media were to censor terrorism, the public would suspect that other things are censored as well. Credibility in the media would decline.

8. Suppression of news on terrorism might leave the public with a false sense of security. People would be unprepared to deal with terrorism when directly faced with it.

9. The lack of public awareness of certain terrorist activities would keep the public from fully understanding the political situation.

10. The feeling of being deprived of vital information might create a public distrust in the political authorities.

11. The assertion by insurgent terrorists that democratic states are not really free would gain added credibility if the freedom of the press were suspended.

Terrorist use of mass media for propaganda

Modern terrorist groups can utilise the mass media for propaganda in various ways:

▶ to instil fear in a mass audience

▶ to polarise public opinion

▶ to gain publicity by agreeing to clandestine interviews

▶ to demand publication of a manifesto

▶ to provoke government over-reaction

▶ to spread false and misleading information

▶ to bring about the release of prisoners

▶ to attract converts and support to a cause

▶ to coerce the media by assaulting journalists

▶ to profit from 'free advertising'

▶ to discredit public officials while being held hostage

▶ to direct public attention by bombing their way onto the front page

▶ to send messages to comrades in another country

▶ to excite the public against the legitimate government

▶ to bolster the terrorist group's morale

▶ to gain the Robin Hood image by fighting 'injustice'

▶ to obtain information on counter-terrorist strategies

▶ to identify future victims

▶ to acquire information about popular support for the terrorist group

▶ to exploit the exaggerated media image of a powerful, omnipotent group.

Tutorial

Progress questions

1. Discuss how the media report terrorism using your own survey of newspapers and television.

2. Is it fair to refer to a 'contagion effect'?

3. Suggest a correct balance between censorship and providing people with news.

Discussion points

1. Is it an exaggeration to say that terrorism is a form of communication?

2. How should censorship be defined in the face of the challenge from revolutionary conflicts?

3. Is propaganda a correct word to use in the context of terrorist use of the media?

Practical assignments

1. Devise a policy on which the media might collectively agree on the issue of terrorism.

2. Consider whether one can differentiate between the press and television reporting of terrorism. Compile a list of key points.

3. How far can one develop a policy of censorship on terrorism, in a democratic society? Compile a list of key points.

5

Intelligence, the Law and Terrorism

One-minute summary – Intelligence is a major issue in the development and progress of revolutionary conflicts. In this chapter we will discuss intelligence and the law, intelligence and terrorism, and intelligence and perception. In particular we will explore:

▶ intelligence and terrorism
▶ the role of League of Nations.
▶ the role of United Nations: 1972 draft convention
▶ acts against terrorism: the purpose.
▶ the European Convention on Human Rights 1950
▶ the European Convention on the Suppression of Terrorism 1976
▶ the Bonn Summit Declaration 1978.

Intelligence and terrorism

Intelligence can be useful against terrorism. It is used for the following:

1. Identifying those involved whatever the level of their involvement, and building a database which can be used to establish patterns of demands and methods which can improve decision-making in times of crisis.

2. Identifying those most at risk and the property most at risk, therefore helping to save lives. Clandestine counter-attacks would be organised (covert action), supply routes established and safe houses and sources of recruits, weapons and finances acquired.

3. Assisting in the development of a counter-propaganda effort targeted either at the support population or those immediately involved, and spreading black propaganda.

4. Seeking to disrupt the solidarity of a group against which an intelligence effort is directed, warning of impending attack and disrupting such attacks. The placement of resources could be influenced by factors such as the police, the military and available hardware.

5. Disrupting the communications network of those involved through interception or the fear of interception.

6. Allowing information to be selectively released to win allies or dissuade hostile powers, and to guide decisions concerning the political reforms which may isolate or discourage the terrorist.

7. Increasing the amount of information available through exchanges with other services and assisting in the management of crisis situations, offering 'battlefield' intelligence as opposed to strategic intelligence.

Intelligence and counter-intelligence

Intelligence information cycle
There are three main stages in the intelligence information cycle:

Collecting information/intelligence
▶ Established lines of communication

▶ Open sources (libraries, newspapers, periodicals)

▶ Criminal information services (Criminal Investigation Department, Federal Bureau of Investigation)

▶ Other intelligence services (military, federal, MI5, MI6, Central Intelligence Agency, foreign intelligence services)

▶ Clandestine agents.

Analysing collected information and intelligence
▶ Relevance

▶ Reliability
▶ Rationality.

Utilising intelligence
▶ Determine its classification
▶ Get information to individuals who are decision-makers
▶ Store the information for later use
▶ Forecast trends and developments
▶ Evaluate any problems
▶ Conduct a threat analysis.

Intelligence and planning
Intelligence can help in the planning of countermeasures:

▶ prevention
▶ control
▶ containment
▶ restoration.

This can be translated into the practical steps of:

▶ effective anti-terrorist laws
▶ central coordinating security
▶ no deals with terrorists
▶ counter propaganda.

Consequences of inadequate intelligence
Intelligence which is inadequate can lead to an inadequate international response due to:

▶ the 'political offences' loophole
▶ intelligence and police cooperation
▶ problems over extradition
▶ the absence of guidelines for a response by Western democracies.

Views of terror

Views of terror can be hard line (hawkish) or soft line (dovish).

Hawks
The hawks argue that terrorism is:

▶ promoted by leftist ideology
▶ leads to the creation of a terrorist international
▶ produces violence which is mindless, senseless and irrational.

Doves
The doves argue that:

▶ terrorists are not all the same (ideologically)
▶ there are links between groups with no commonality
▶ there is a shaky contagion hypothesis
▶ there is a moral duty to protect nations
▶ the granting of asylum is useful
▶ terrorism is the politics of desperation and the refuge of the weak.

Subversion

Subversives, or those who wish to undermine society, must:

▶ demoralise the government's police force
▶ destabilise the government's army
▶ widen areas of support
▶ successfully propagate a clear and unequivocal aim.

Whether deterrence deters such subversives depends upon:

▶ how many ransoms are demanded
▶ retaliation by government moves against terrorists
▶ publicity associated with kidnapping
▶ terrorist and government repression
▶ the value of hostages

▶ if a 'no ransom' policy is successful, terrorists can engage in other violent action.

Subversives are hostile to the rule of law, namely:

▶ the independence of the judiciary
▶ freedom from arbitrary arrest
▶ proper legal representation.

The League of Nations

The interwar years (1919–39)

Systematic terrorism was found mainly on the fringes of the budding fascist movements or among their precursors such as the Freikorps in Germany and certain French fascist groups.

There were a few spectacular political assassinations, such as those of Liebknecht and Luxemburg in 1919 and Rathenau in 1922. The assassination of King Alexander of Yugoslavia and the French foreign minister Barthou in Marseilles in 1934 was clearly a case of international terrorism in which at least four governments were involved. The League of Nations intervened, resolutions were passed and committees were established with a view to combating terrorism on an international basis.

Convention on the Suppression of Terrorism

The 1937 League of Nations Conference on the Suppression of Terrorism produced a convention for that purpose. The convention never received sufficient ratification to be enacted and so remained a dead issue. Such exercises were quite futile for the obvious reason that, although some governments were opposed to terror, others favoured it as long as it served their purposes. As we shall see, three decades later, the UN faced a similar situation.

The Convention had a number of shortcomings.

▶ The document required all signatories to make acts of terrorism committed on their territories, criminal offences.

▶ Signatories were required to either extradite or punish persons who committed these offences abroad.

Acts of terrorism were defined in Article 2 to include:

▶ causing death, grievous bodily harm or loss of liberty to heads of state, their spouses and others holding public office

▶ wilful destruction of public property

▶ acts endangering the lives of members of the public.

Article 3 specified further that conspiracy to commit the above acts, and incitement and assistance in performing such acts, were likewise criminal offences.

Thus the attempted assassination of Hitler and the execution of Mussolini would readily have qualified as internationally condemned terrorist acts under the proposed Convention, while post-Second World War liberation movements would have been defined as terroristic under it. Moreover, broadcasting to an oppressed people to encourage them to rise against a regime that was exploiting them would have been condemned as an incitement to commit international crime.

The League Convention clearly attempted to perpetuate the pre-Second World War status quo and manifested a willingness to label any future revolutionary or national liberation movement as terrorist. By 1945, however, it was clear that the League's work in this area would be ineffective in dealing with terrorist excesses and, more pertinently, in getting international consensus with regard to the suppression of terrorism.

The United Nations

Since 1945 – and more especially since 1985 – the UN has been increasingly focused on issues germane to international terror. In October 1985 the Security Council of the UN condemned terrorism in all its forms and more particularly all acts of hostage-taking and abduction. Nevertheless many observers have suggested limitations to and deficiencies in the efforts of the United Nations to impede international terrorist activities.

International law against various forms of terrorism has to be strengthened both substantively and procedurally. However, compliance will be imperfect as long as nation-states remain the world power centres, and as long as many of them are prepared to flout or ignore international law when it suits their immediate national goals.

Law enforcement is not in the hands of the UN. It must be the job of governments. If not all governments are prepared to enforce the law and to apprehend and punish the criminals then those governments that are ready to act must do so decisively and cooperatively.

A government can be excluded from cooperative efforts to enforce the law only by itself. Action is required not only against the terrorists themselves but also against those governments which assist, protect and harbour them.

Two decades ago, the UN adopted a resolution which contained a number of useful provisions regarding possible future measures toward combating international terrorism, in particular the request by the Secretary-General to build up a body of national legislation regarding international terrorism. Such information would be useful to states wishing to structure their law and policy so as to combat terrorism effectively while safeguarding fundamental human rights.

Measures adopted in general have had a specific, narrow focus. They have covered only a particular type of target or victim – civil aviation and diplomats – or a particular manifestation of terrorism, such as hostage-taking.

There is a need for the UN to come to grips with other facets of international terrorism:

► the war of assassination by states against their enemies abroad which threatens international peace and security

► the movement against gross violations of human rights such as torture, that create an environment in which terrorism may spread.

The UN realises that the justness of a cause does not excuse the use of terrorist methods. All states have an interest in suppressing actions of violence and whatever the end, the means cannot legitimately include the exploding of bombs in towns, the taking of hostages, the killing of diplomats, the hijacking of planes or the sending of letter bombs.

Definitional disagreements have severely hindered UN efforts to make any substantive progress on international cooperation against terrorism beyond very specific agreements on individual aspects of the problem, such as diplomatic security and civil aviation matters.

Draft convention to suppress international terrorism

A draft convention to suppress international terrorism was put before the UN by the USA in September 1972.

▶ The major, and limited, intent was to require countries to either prosecute or extradite those engaging in the exporting of terrorism.

▶ An offender must intend to damage the interests of or to obtain concessions from a state or international organisation.

▶ Prohibited acts include killing, causing grievous bodily harm and kidnapping.

▶ Acts are defined as international offences if they are committed outside the offender's own country, and
   – also outside the country against which they are intended;
   – within the country against which they are intended but against persons who are not nationals of that state.

The main advantage was the narrow scope makes it much less subject to criticism for being oppressive to unorthodox political change. The main disadvantage was that having defined its goals so narrowly, the convention was seen to be far-fetched and irrelevant. For example, an Irish offender bombing a London café inhabited only by English people would be exempt. The convention steered clear of ideological conflicts but the American authorship doomed it from the start.

The basic principles of the limited goals were: fight your enemies in your country or theirs, and do not export your grievances to distant places where innocent persons are likely to be affected.

Today any revival of this effort remains unlikely. Despite the existence of some historical and legal insights into the nature of modern terrorism, there has been little success in reaching an 'internationally' acceptable definition.

Legislation against terrorism

The aim of such legislation is to prevent the fugitive offender from classing his or her action as a political offence or an offence inspired by political motives. Typically:

▶ There are limitations on procedural protections.

▶ Powers in such legislation are temporary.

▶ Legislation passed in periods of crisis is not adequately debated.

▶ Legislation has a greater limitation on civil liberties than is required to combat terror.

Three examples of legislation

European Convention on Human Rights 1950
This Convention examines complaints against any violation of human rights, and is germane to curbing terroristic and revolutionary violence. There is a right to life protected by law; torture and slavery are prohibited. There is a right to liberty and a fair hearing, under the protection of international law; and there is a right to privacy and freedom.

European Convention on Suppression of Terrorism 1976
This measure can facilitate the extradition and prosecution of perpetrators of terrorist acts even though such acts might be

politically motivated and therefore excluded from extradition arrangements. Various articles refer to:

▶ response to hijacking, bombing, kidnapping, acts of violence against life

▶ jurisdiction over offences, crime problems, interpretation of the Convention

▶ specification of territories and refusal of extradition and denunciation by states.

The Bonn Summit Declaration 1978
This stated that governments should intensify their efforts to combat international terrorism. Where countries refuse to prosecute hijackers then governments should take immediate action to cease all flights. The Declaration was signed by Canada, France, West Germany, Italy, Japan, the UK and the USA.

Tutorial

Progress questions
1. State how democracies can effectively deter terrorism without draconian measures.

2. How did the League of Nations try to solve the problem of terrorism?

3. Critically appraise the effectiveness of anti-terrorist legislation.

Discussion points
1. No matter how effective the intelligence against terrorism, terrorism cannot be defeated. Do you agree?

2. From your own knowledge, are the British effective in counter-terrorism?

3. Why has the UN had relatively little success in combating terrorism?

4. What criteria would you use for stating whether you are a dove or a hawk in the consideration of terrorism issues?

Practical assignment

1. Formulate a deterrence policy for a government fighting terrorism.

6

Aspects of Global Terrorism

One-minute summary – In an age of ever more powerful technology and communications, human society is becoming increasingly globalised. The trend towards globalisation is affecting political, economic, cultural and social life almost everywhere. In this chapter we will discuss the various features of global terrorism. In particular we will explore terrorism in three key geographical areas of the world:

▶ Europe, with particular attention to Northern Ireland
▶ the United States of America
▶ the Middle East.

Europe

As with other areas of the world, terror in Europe is not value free and has international dimensions, by reason of its locale, the aims of terrorist acts, and the terrorist's nationality, the source of arms and the links with other terrorists outside a given country.

In Western Europe liberal democracies have coped with various levels of terrorist activity:

▶ *West Germany pre-1989* – terrorist activity was designed to challenge and undermine the claim to legitimacy of the elected government.

▶ *Northern Ireland* – terrorism has sought to undermine the authorities in office.

▶ *Netherlands* – terrorist activity by the South Moluccans was goal-centred and aimed at redressing long-standing political grievances.

▶ *Italy* – the goals were diffuse and drawn from both ends of the political spectrum.

▶ *France* – here there was a lower level of political violence with terrorists having a wide variety of goals and disparate ideological roots. Regional groups have engaged in symbolic bombing campaigns against symbols of state domination and rivals have employed their own levels of violence.

'Ideology' can be a grandiose term to ascribe to the network of tactics and goals that has underlined the terrorist's campaign on Europe. Not only are short-term aims and long-term goals difficult to distinguish, but these nationalist ideologies weave together divergent threads of argument into a messy amalgam of ideas. A core theme of the left-wing groups in Europe was hostility to American influence and the liberal-democratic social and economic structure.

In spite of the European Convention on the Suppression of Terrorism it is clear that progress towards a common European Union policy against terrorism has proved highly problematic and the adoption of further measures has become increasingly more difficult as the EU has expanded in size. Yet terrorism represents a significant threat to shared liberal-democratic values.

Effective anti-terrorist action therefore of necessity requires some degree of international cooperation, be it only the willingness of a state of refuge to extradite terrorist offenders to states that are willing and have the jurisdiction to try them.

There is no general obligation imposed by international law upon a state either to try or to extradite fugitive offenders within its borders. Criminal jurisdiction will not solve problems that result in terrorism, but it can have a role to play in an overall strategy, particularly a strategy involving international cooperation. Traditionally in Western Europe, extradition (the formal surrender of fugitive offenders) is a judicial procedure in which the various requirements of extradition law have to be proved to the satisfaction of a court.

Europe as a target for terrorism
Europe has been a tempting target for international terrorists because:

▶ It contains large contingents of ethnic minorities – Croatians, Palestinians and Armenians to name a few.

▶ The primary targeted countries are in or near Europe, for example Israel, Turkey and the former Yugoslavia.

▶ The continent is geographically compact.

▶ There is a broad target area of certain groups of people, for example some of the world's most prominent personalities and Jews.

▶ The publicity spotlight is brighter and more intense.

▶ There exists an indigenous terror threat which has toppled governments (Turkey), shaken others (Spain), and challenges the political system (Italy and Northern Ireland).

▶ There are strained bilateral relations between many countries.

TREVI

TREVI was set up as an inter-governmental forum in 1976 and stands for 'Terrorism Radicalism, Extremism and International Violence'. Its goal is to facilitate cooperation at a practical, operational level against terrorism, drug-trafficking and other serious crime and public order problems.

Working groups exist on terrorism, on public order issues, on serious and organised international crime and on police and security issues with regard to the free movement of peoples.

The TREVI group have generally accepted that terrorism should be treated as a crime and not, selectively, as the pursuit of international politics. One of the TREVI group's more difficult decisions was to solve the problem of imposing uniformly strict airport security, visa requirements and border controls.

Following TREVI, the Palma Report (1989) identified terrorism, drug-trafficking and other illicit trafficking, and improved police cooperation as being of particular concern. The Schengen Agreement covering European frontiers and the 1992 processes linked to a wider European Union placed demands on bodies unused to trans-frontier consultation, coordination and cooperation. In fighting terrorism it was clear that the parameters of internal and external security would have to be mapped out.

Ireland

Chronology of significant events

Below is a chronology of significant events in Irish history with particular relevance to Ulster (1690–1987).

1690	Battle of the Boyne.
1916	Easter Rising.
1921	Irish Free State established and Ireland is partitioned.
1922	Civil War in Ireland; Irish Republican Army goes underground.
1939–45	IRA campaign against the British military.
1956–62	IRA border war with Ulster.
1967	Northern Ireland Civil Rights Association formed. Issues include: – discrimination in job and housing – gerrymandering of voting districts to exclude Catholics – voting which is based on property ownership – police brutality.
1969	A split develops in the IRA and the Provisional Wing is formed. British troops arrive in Ulster.
1972	Bloody Sunday: UK begins direct rule of Ulster and establishes a policy of internment.
1974	Irish National Liberation Army emerges advocating armed warfare with Britain.
1975	Sectarian violence escalates with creation of Protestant Death Squads; IRA retaliates.
1980	Assassination of Lord Mountbatten and 18 British soldiers.
1981	Hunger strike begins at Maze Prison and ten die.
1982	Bombing campaign continues in United Kingdom; Crocus Street ambush.
1983–84	Escapes from Maze Prison; London bombings; attempt on life of British Prime Minister Thatcher by bomb in Brighton hotel.
1985	Bombing of police barracks; Anglo-Irish Treaty; Sinn Fein wins 11% of Catholic vote in Ulster.
1986	Protestant backlash to Anglo-Irish Treaty and United States ratifies new extradition treaty with United Kingdom.
1987	Eight Provisional IRA terrorists killed in shoot-out with British military in South Armagh.

Can the power of the IRA be eroded?
The authorities have to:

▶ resist demands that the visible strength of the army be increased

▶ use both Irish police forces and armies to improve border security

▶ apply money directly to the devastated Republican areas of Belfast and Londonderry.

The United States of America

Although the USA has been the primary target of a variety of foreign terrorist organisations, it has remained relatively insulated from these escalations of terrorist violence. Until the events of 11 September 2001 more Americans had been killed overseas as a result of terrorist bombings than within its own borders, and this included the Oklahoma bombing of April 1995.

Reasons for the low level of terrorism
What are the reasons for the low level of terrorism in the USA?

▶ The country is not politically polarised and has traditionally been a two-party system, the parties differing little in actual substance from one another.

▶ Terrorism has been ineffective because of the country's unparalleled upward economic and social mobility which provides opportunities for social and economic advancement.

▶ The country is a politically absorbent society. Aspects of American politics have reflected its ethnic diversity and immigrants have been absorbed.

▶ The geographical size of the USA inhibits widespread violence and it is less easy for terrorists to enter or leave the country than, say, Europe.

Terrorist organisations in the USA

Four types of terrorist organisation exist in the USA:

- ethnic separatist and emigré groups;
- left-wing radical organisations;
- right-wing racist, anti-authority and extreme survivalist type groups;
- Islamic fundamentalist groups.

American-based terrorists concentrate on bombing which provides a dramatic way of drawing attention to the terrorists and their causes. Members of these groups are more skilled with weapons than other terrorists in the USA, and are well trained in survival techniques and in living rough. The events of 11 September 2001 have led to a re-examination of terrorist groups in America.

The Oklahoma City bomb, April 1995

As in the Middle East, so in the USA the use of violence is justified by theological imperative as a means to overthrow a reviled secular government and attain both racial purification and religious redemption. The 1995 bombing had the hallmark of an indigenous violent, Christian white supremacist movement that had been active for some years. The perpetrator of this act was Timothy McVeigh, and 160 were killed. A year earlier at the Branch Davidian compound in Waco, Texas, 74 persons were killed, including 24 children. The Branch included white supremacists.

Lone terrorists

A recent fear facing the United States has come from lone terrorists, such as the so-called 'unabomber' Theodore Kaczynski, who allegedly conducted a lone 17-year terrorist campaign. He targeted persons associated with either universities or the airline industry, and in the process killed three people and wounded 23 others using simple yet ingeniously constructed home-made bombs sent through the post. He argued that he could restrict his campaign if a major American paper printed his entire message against technology, modernity and the destruction of the environment. Kaczynski was arrested shortly afterwards. He was a bizarre lone individual, now in prison, who epitomised the terrorist's symbiotic relationship with the media, yet one who quite simply dispatched home-made bombs made form ordinary materials through the post, allegedly from a remote log cabin in Montana.

On a global scale, this showed that terrorism had become accessible to anyone with a grievance, an agenda, a purpose or any idiosyncratic combination.

International terrorism

Two years earlier in February 1993 the bombing of the World Trade Centre in New York (using 1,200 pounds of combustible material) killed six people and injured 1,000 others and was possibly the first case in the USA concerning international terrorism. It shattered any illusion that the USA is immune from the hand of new fanatical terrorists. The Centre was a major symbol of US wealth, power and prestige. The choice of the target, which houses many of the country's most important corporations, was not merely opportunistic. Although the plot may have been technically flawed, it was socially and politically shrewd in making the point that the very nerve centre of the US economy, located in a major population centre, was vulnerable to the crippling blows of a dedicated group of believers.

The Middle East

Few areas in the world can compare with the complexities of terrorism in the Middle East. Turmoil in the region results from conflicts old and new and from deeply felt religious, familial and national convictions. It is a geographic region of immense economic importance and since 1945 it not only has been the scene of a series of conventional wars but has also become closely associated with the growth of modern terrorism. Although most fighting is about internal issues, terrorism has spilled over into international affairs.

Characteristics of society in the Middle East
▶ The current structure of Middle Eastern geography and

political rule is a direct result of the nineteenth-century European imperial influence in the region and the outcomes of the First World War.

▶ There is a deep-rooted antagonism between Arab and Jew, on familial, religious and geographic grounds.

▶ Arabs and Palestinians in particular do not hold a monopoly on terrorism.

▶ The religious differences in the region have developed over centuries, and fanaticism in any one of them can spawn violence.

Terrorism in the Middle East today

Since the Second World War the Middle East has been a tense area. Increasingly, terrorism has become a standard method of military operations, in particular after the Six Day War between Egypt and Israel in 1967.

In 1964 the Palestinian Liberation Organisation was created, and in 1993 it renounced terrorism. However, violent and horrific acts of terrorism occurred in the intervening years. Some groups denounced the PLO's ordering of terrorism, most notably the Islamic fundamentalist group Hamas, while others embraced the PLO's decision.

A similar reaction has occurred in Israel where one political party has endorsed the peace plans (the Socialist party), and another prepares for a potential war (the Likud party).

Middle East peace is a very fragile process and terrorism is a wild card which can undermine the most constructive of diplomacy, even after peace treaties have been signed and implemented.

Tutorial

Progress questions

1. Why has terrorism been particularly effective in France and Germany?

2. What are the difficulties in reaching a common European Union position on fighting terrorism?

3. Why do terrorists target prominent people?

4. Why is the Irish question so dogged by historical problems?

5. How far is terrorism in the Middle East part of a wider malaise in the area?

Discussion points
1. Do you believe power can be eroded in the Irish Republican Army?

2. Account for the different level of development of terrorism in the United States compared with Europe.

3. The very nature of societies in the Middle East means terroristic violence will always occur. Do you agree?

Practical assignments
1. Which European country do you think is most afflicted by revolutionary violence and why?

2. If you were a TREVI forum member, how would you reform the organisation?

3. Critically assess the table of significant events in Northern Ireland and decide which factors have had most effect.

7

Psychological Issues: Kidnapping and Hostage-Taking

One-minute summary – In this chapter we will examine the key psychological issues relating to terrorism and the effects of kidnapping and hostage-taking. In particular we will explore:

► the modern terrorist mindset
► the unique nature of terrorism strategy
► the inner landscape of terrorism
► exploitation of fear: kidnapping and terrorism
► propaganda, subversion and threats to free societies
► hostage events and hostage-taking.

The modern terrorist mindset

The wrath of the terrorist is rarely uncontrolled. Contrary to popular belief and media depiction, most terrorism is neither crazed nor capricious. Rather terrorist attacks are both premeditated and carefully planned. The terrorist act reflects the terrorist group's particular aims and motivations, fits its resources and capabilities and takes into account the resources and capabilities of the 'target audience' at which the act is directed. The tactics and targets of various terrorist movements as well as the weapons they favour are therefore shaped by a group's ideology, its internal organisational dynamics and the personalities of its key members, as well as a variety of internal and external stimuli.

Left-wing terrorists
The overriding tactical – and ethical – imperative for left-wing terrorists has been the deliberate tailoring of violent acts to appeal to their perceived 'constituencies'. Left-wing terrorists' use of

violence has been heavily constrained. Their self-styled crusade for social justice is typically directed against governmental or commercial institutions, or specific individuals who they believe represent capitalist exploitation and repression. Left-wing violence tends to be discriminate, selective and limited. Consider the case of wealthy industrialists like Martin Schleyer, kidnapped and murdered by the German Red Army Faction in 1977, and leading parliamentarians, such as the Italian Prime Minister, Aldo Moro, kidnapped and murdered by the Italian Red Brigade in 1978.

Ethno-nationalist/separatist terrorists

Ethno-nationalist/separatist groups see themselves as a revolutionary vanguard. They use violence to draw the attention of fellow members of their national or ethnic group to the inequities imposed upon them by the ruling government and the need for communal resistance and rebellion. One example is the Basque group Euzkadi Ta Askatasuna (Basque Freedom and Homeland).

The more successful ethno-nationalist/separatist terrorist organisation will be able to determine an effective level of violence that is at once 'tolerable' for the local populace, tacitly acceptable to international opinion and sufficiently modulated not to provoke massive governmental crackdown and reaction. For example, the Irish Republican Army has demonstrably mastered this synchronisation of tactics to strategy. Republican strategy has required a certain level of violence – but only enough to distort the private and public life of the North and to make sure that the military arm was properly exercised. Members of the security forces have been targeted in preference to the terrorists' avowed enemies in some rival indigenous community.

Even when terrorist actions are not as deliberate or discriminating, and when their purpose is in fact to kill innocent civilians, the target is still regarded as 'justified' because it represents the terrorist's defined 'enemy'.

Right-wing terrorism

Right-wing terrorism has often been characterised as the least discriminating, most senseless type of contemporary political violence. It has, for example, targeted immigrants, refugees, guest workers and other foreigners in many European countries.

The European groups share many similarities (racism, anti-semitism, xenophobia and a hatred of liberal government) with their American counterparts, but differ in legitimisation and justification. US groups are more religious while the European groups are avowedly secular. The latter have hardly changed in their target choice – refugee shelters and immigrant workers hostels, anarchist houses and political party offices.

Right-wing violence is based on a deliberate policy of intimidating the general public into acceding to specific demands or pressures. They tend to seek to keep the violence they commit within the bounds of what the ruling government will tolerate without undertaking massive repressive actions against the terrorists themselves.

Religious terrorism

For religious terrorist movements violence still has an instrumental purpose but, unlike secular terrorists, it is also often an end in itself – a sacred duty executed in direct response to some theological demand or imperative, as with the Lebanese Shi'a terrorists.

For religious terrorists there are fewer constraints on the actual infliction of violence and the category of targets/enemies is much more open-ended. The willingness of religious terrorists to contemplate such wholesale acts of violence is a direct reflection of the fact that, unlike their secular counterparts, they do not seek to appeal to any person or authority other than their own god or religious figures, and therefore feel little need to regulate their violence.

The unique nature of terrorism strategy

▶ It is avowedly political in aims and motives.

▶ It is violent – or threatens violence.

▶ It is designed to have far-reaching psychological repercussions beyond the immediate victim or target.

▶ It is conducted by an organisation with an identifiable chain of command or conspiratorial cell structure (whose members wear no uniform or identifying insignia).

▶ It is perpetuated by a subnational group or non-state entity.

The inner landscape of terrorism

What makes terrorists tick?
While there is no single mindset, certain mental traits are widely observable:

▶ *self-righteousness* – a dogmatic assertiveness of their own positions, and intolerance of others' views;

▶ *frustration* – impatience with a society perceived to be oppressive;

▶ *oversimplification* – a fanatical, black and white view of the world;

▶ *isolation* – loneliness and an inability to function well in social groups;

▶ *utopianism* – a feeling that a vaguely defined, perfect society is just around the corner;

▶ *coldbloodedness* – a willingness to murder ruthlessly, seeing victims as mere objects.

A typical terrorist
A typical terrorist will feel that violence is morally justifiable, backed by a political necessity for all terrorist actions. Terrorists are capable of extraordinary bloodshed, reprisal killings and elements of surprise and ruthlessness.

The incitement of popular support and mass arousal can help in highlighting the repressive side of government, and targets can be attacked to incapacitate governments. Secrecy is necessary if acts are to be systematically planned and deliberately executed, and also if acts have limited scope and are persistently accomplished.

What makes a terrorist?
The range of personalities attracted to the terrorist fold is very wide and varied. Responses to life as a terrorist are equally varied.

But there is a commonality of experience among individuals and groups:

- ▶ There is a feeling of restlessness between 'actions'.

- ▶ There is a feeling of being trapped.

- ▶ Planning and target selection are often haphazard.

- ▶ There are worries about declining effectiveness and numbers of sympathisers.

- ▶ There are strong differences of opinion over means and ends.

- ▶ Pressures, stresses and tensions are ever-present.

- ▶ There are often unconscious patricidal impulses.

- ▶ Personality traits are linked to 'rigidity' – an inability to form meaningful relationships and a total rejection of the entire social order.

- ▶ Death-seeking and death-confronting behaviour is manifested.

- ▶ There is a feeling of emptiness and an inability to enjoy anything.

- ▶ Actions are sparked and guided by an ideology of ideas and objectives that go beyond personal interests and have some altruistic or idealistic appearance.

- ▶ There has to be a desire to actively fight that society with violence from inside a like-minded group

- ▶ A would-be terrorist/guerrilla has to be acceptable to the elite and special organisation which he or she is about to join.

- ▶ The individual or group wishes to bring about change through instant action.

- ▶ There is a hyper-worldly awareness of the sufferings and injustices of the world at large.

▶ Once in a group it is difficult for a terrorist to leave without putting his or her life on the line, both with the group and with the authorities.

▶ Attention-seeking is a key aspect of their identity.

The exploitation of fear

Terrorism can exploit fear to the full.

▶ Terrorism is an uncertain and indirect strategy that employs the weapon of fear to make governments react. Fright can paralyse the will, befuddle the mind and exhaust the strength of an adversary.

▶ Terrorism can make heroes out of gunmen, and thereby rally popular support to their cause.

▶ Terrorist provocations can also make policemen into villains. It is this ability to use the strength of repression against itself, in many different ways, that has enabled terrorist strategies to succeed in many situations that have been described as colonialist in the modern world.

Examples

The Irgun Zvai Leumi
The terrorist exploitation of fear can best be illustrated by the Irgun Zvai Leumi, a 1,500-strong band of Jewish militants in what was in 1945 the British mandated territory of Palestine. Unlike the Palestinian Jewish community the Irgun wanted independence then and there in order to open up the country to refugees from Hitler's Europe. They got what they wanted when they wanted it by doing things in their own way. The strategy was ingenious to the extent that the Irgun played a big part in getting the British to withdraw. Its ingenuity lay in using an opponent's own strength against him. The adversary was made to be afraid, and then predictably he would react to his fear by increasing the bulk of his strength, and then the sheer weight of that bulk would drag him down.

The Algerian National Liberation Front
In Algeria in the 1950s the nationalist rebel group, the National Liberation Front (the FLN), developed another method of using the strength of the occupying power against itself. Their method was to induce that strength to be used as a form of persuasion. Would the indigenous population be convinced by the French government that Algeria was not a separate country? Or could they be persuaded by the FLN to change their minds and think of themselves as a nation?

By itself terror can accomplish nothing in terms of political goals: it can only aim at obtaining a response that will achieve those goals for it. What the FLN did was to goad the French into reacting in such a way as to demonstrate the unreality of the claim that there was no distinct Algerian nation. Unlike the Irgun, the FLN did not set out to campaign merely against property, it attacked people associated with the French colonial regime. The French in turn threw away the potential support of Muslim Algeria because they were sceptical of the possibility that it could be obtained. Once the sympathies of the population had shifted to its side, the FLN was able to outgrow mere terrorism and to organise a campaign of guerrilla warfare.

The importance of strategy
Many political successes have been scored by the strategy of terrorism in the past four decades. This is in no small part due to the miscomprehension of strategy by its opponents. They have failed to focus on the crucial issue of how the opponents' response affects the political goals of the terrorists. Discussion has centred on the criminal justice system and issues of prevention and punishment. Terrorism is the indirect strategy that wins or loses only in terms of how you respond to it. If one chooses to respond in a way different from that which the terrorists desire, they will fail to achieve their objectives.

Today's world seems to breed more and more terrorists. They appear to thrive and multiply everywhere in the world, bomb or machine gun in hand, motivated by political fantasies and hallucinations, fully convinced that their slaughter of the innocents will somehow usher in a political utopia for mankind.

A continuing subculture of terrorism

Succeeding generations of terrorists replace those arrested or killed. They acquire a following of active supporters, sympathisers, lawyers, propagandists and chroniclers. All in some way depend on the survival of the terrorist group and the continuation of its activities. It may become a political underworld that is able to survive the fate of any specific terrorist group. It can develop its own service industries providing illegal documents and weapons as well as fences for stolen cash or ransoms. The people in this subculture are:

▶ absolutists or 'true believers' – uncompromising, action prone, impatient persons who may seek instant gratification via their actions

▶ gun freaks – abnormally fascinated with firearms and explosives, not generally suicidal but persons who might be described as 'risk seekers'.

A psychiatric view
Psychiatrists say that terrorists in such a subculture suffer from:

▶ a feeling of anonymity
▶ a sense of deprivation
▶ a sense of powerlessness
▶ a feeling that one's self-esteem and masculinity have been assaulted consistently
▶ the desire not only for attention but intimacy with powerful figures of society.

Some psychiatrists argue that some terrorists are sick persons, mentally ill or physically impaired who feel genuine grievances justify their actions.

How terrorists decide to do what they do is uncertain. One cannot be sure why a terrorist group may decide to assassinate instead of kidnap, how they select their target, and whether and when they may escalate their violence.

Operational patterns

▶ Each terrorist group has its own repertoire, its own style of operations, its own modus operandi.

▶ The particular operational pattern of a terrorist group depends upon whether they are university dropouts, or ex-soldiers or from other occupational backgrounds.

▶ Culture may determine actions.

▶ Ideology may dictate the victims and targets.

▶ Mostly the groups operate below their technological ceiling.

The mix of types in terrorist organisations can comprise the 'ideologue', the 'soldier' and the 'thug'. All types concentrate on the negative aspects of what they see before them to the point that any alternative would be more desirable than that which exists. A line of propaganda can be developed which insists that things are now so intolerably bad that destruction must take priority over reform or construction.

Within the mix of types it is the least mature group which tends to pose the most dangerous and immediate threat because it is likely to be reckless with violence.

Propaganda, subversion and the threat to free societies

▶ There is a seriousness of purpose and an attention to detail.

▶ Propaganda without credibility would lose its effectiveness.

▶ Propaganda theory tells the terrorist that his chances for causing people to make drastic changes in their normal behaviour lie in appealing to the most basic of their 'psychological needs' as they stand at the time the appeal is made.

Terrorism is one behaviour pattern in the whole panoply of revolutionary actions, although on a world basis, its importance within any society is inversely related to the revolutionary potential of the people.

Terrorism represents an act of weakness rather than burgeoning strength, and its occurrence is not likely in historical settings and social structures where revolutionary potential is less prevalent. The main danger facing terrorism is that of being ignored, of receiving insufficient publicity and of losing the image of a desperate freedom fighter. Therefore to succeed, terrorist demands have to be realistic, i.e. limited in character. Terrorists do not know what to do about declining readiness on the part of governments to be intimidated by acts of terror.

Terrorist intransigence
The intransigence of terrorists is often a self-fulfilling result of the rigidity of government moves. These often follow a 'textbook' approach for dealing with criminal behaviour which does not permit any exploration of the variability within the terrorist event itself. Rigidity tends to breed rigidity between the terrorist and society. The terrorists' impossible demands are followed by ultimatums on the part of government.

The tendency to get out of hand
Terrorism is a weapon that can and does get out of hand among those who use it. By initiating and participating in terrorism, leaders are releasing human potential for destructiveness over which they do not have full control. The terrorists themselves can never predict the level and intensity of violence to which they will be subjected either as possible killers and/or as victims.

Threats to free societies exploited by subcultures
▶ Private coercion of groups/individuals to bring about change

▶ Derangement of the functions of government

▶ The nature of totalitarianism in stifling freedom

▶ Constitutional voting to bring about change.

Targets who can also be subversives from the subculture viewpoint
▶ Classes of people unfriendly to many

▶ Members of non-communist parties

▶ Persons with foreign contacts

▶ Ethnic groups

▶ Persons with family ties.

Modernisation and the propensity for violence

▶ In a *subjective sense*, there is a revolution of rising expectations, a loss of faith in normative systems and authority, and pseudo humanitarianism based on the perfectibility of human nature, exaggerated compassion for criminals and a negation of the philosophy of responsibility.

▶ In an *objective* way, there is a rising complexity, interdependence and dynamism in modern societies providing sensitive targets for terrorism.

▶ There has been a rapid advance in the destructiveness and effectiveness of modern weaponry available for violence and terrorism as well as for legitimate use.

▶ Advances in the efficiency of transportation and communication provide a basis for intelligence, mobility and access to broad publicity for both terrorism and law enforcement agencies.

The opportunity for violence

The opportunity for violence has to be considered in two ways:

1. The extent and probability of the success of violence and terror
   - social density and the close interdependence of modern communities provide excellent targets for acts of violence and terrorism
   - the effectiveness of weaponry increases the probability of success
   - the availability of rapid transportation, advanced communication systems and increased mobility ensure an element of surprise
   - television and other media provide publicity.

2. The risk and cost of apprehension and punishment – permissiveness and leniency in apprehension and conviction caused by the philosophy of pseudo humanitarianism has lowered the risk and cost of violence and terrorism, thus expanding the opportunity for violence.

Hostage events and hostage-taking

Hostage events

There are two forms of response to hostage events: normal and pathological.

Normal response

▶ Outcry – in the form of fear, sadness, anger and rage.

▶ Denial – 'this cannot be happening to me'.

▶ Intrusion – voluntary thoughts of the event.

▶ Coming to terms – working through and facing the reality of the situation.

▶ Completion – or going on with life.

Pathological response

▶ Overwhelmed – emotional reaction of panic and fear.

▶ Extreme avoidance – using drugs and alcohol to avoid pain.

▶ Flooded states – disturbing nightmares and thoughts of the event.

▶ Psychosomatic responses – developing new ailments.

▶ Character distortions – long-term distortions of ability.

Hostage-taking

Hostages are persons delivered to, kept or taken by an enemy as a pledge for the fulfilment of certain conditions, in particular cash remuneration or financial ransom. Hostage-takers fall into three main groups:

▶ *Criminal* – fleeing felon, prison inmate involved in riots, extortionist or kidnapper.

▶ *Political terrorist* – seeking media recognition for a cause, a social protester, a religious zealot, seeking vengeance, an aircraft hijacker, the state as a hostage-taker.

▶ *Psychotic* – the mentally deranged, the suicidal, the angry, those seeking personal recognition, those who are estranged from their family.

Hostage negotiation: the policy debate

'No ransom' position
▶ No capitulation to terrorism is permitted.
▶ Terrorists are international.

Flexible response position
▶ No common tactics/strategy may be formulated.
▶ Terrorists are human.
▶ Political asylum may be granted.

No ransom versus negotiation argument – does deterrence deter?
▶ Those who demand the prisoners' freedom focus adverse publicity on the government.

▶ Those who demand ransoms put targets in a bad light.

▶ Many attacks are made in retaliation for governmental moves against terrorist organisations.

▶ A group may engage in kidnapping to publicise an overall ideology.

▶ Some kidnappings can cause disruption and affect society's expectations of punishment and order.

▶ Terrorists provoke government repression against themselves.

▶ A hostage may have some value to those who have seized him.

▶ An incident may represent an individual's personal

affirmation of solidarity with the norms of the terrorist group.

▶ The threat of kidnapping is part of the urban terrorist's overall strategy.

▶ If the 'no ransom' policy stopped terrorist incidents then terrorists would engage in other types of violent action (non-hostage).

'No ransom' position

▶ Terrorists are all the same – they have a leftist ideology and employ the same tactics.

▶ Due to their links we are seeing the creation of a terrorist international: they share the same funding sources, hold worldwide meetings and conduct joint operations.

▶ If one grants that terrorists are not all the same then it is difficult to collect data at the scene of an incident to enable bargaining to be adapted to the circumstances.

▶ Capitulation encourages others – in isolated incidents the converse is true.

▶ One must remove the temptation to kidnap diplomats by denying such rewards.

▶ It is morally wrong to give in to demands of groups engaging in terrorist acts.

▶ It is the government's responsibility to protect political prisoners.

▶ A stated policy cannot countenance giving in to terrorist demands.

Flexible response position

▶ Terrorists are not all the same and do not react the same way in hostage situations:
   – they differ in ideology and purpose in the choice of terrorism

- they differ in tactics
- they do not hold the same views on the sanctity of life
- they rarely double-cross bargainers.

▶ Links between groups do not lead to commonality of tactics, strategy, perceptions or motivation.
  - Rarely do terrorists attend relevant international meetings.
  - The Palestine Liberation Organisation, for example, is split on the sanctity of life, tactics and strategy.
  - Many terrorist groups fight primary terrorist groups.
  - Nation states have many links in trade and communications.

▶ Data at the site of an incident provide clues on how to conduct negotiations.

▶ The contagion hypothesis rests on shaky evidence.

▶ Governments have a moral duty to protect nationals.

▶ Terrorists care about what happens to them after an incident.

▶ Granting asylum is a time-honoured practice.

▶ The politics of desperation are the last refuges of the weak.

Kidnapping

Kidnapping – the seizure and forcibly carrying away of any person – has been used for many generations. The rise of gangsterism in the 1920s led to a massive growth of kidnapping in the USA, and there has been strong Italian connection with the growth of kidnapping in many American cities. Italy has the highest incidence of kidnapping in Europe and there are strong links between the American and Italian Mafia.

Purpose and form
For contemporary terrorists, kidnapping is a dramatic act.

▶ The capture and detention of a prominent person has served numerous ends, including publicity, the release of colleagues being held as political prisoners and the receipt of substantial funds in ransom payments.

▶ Many terrorist groups have relied on the prolonged detention of their kidnap victims, thus enjoying sustained media attention and causing embarrassment to governments.

▶ Kidnapping of famous people can provide more media attention than a single robbery, bombing or assassination.

▶ The eventual release of a hostage can serve to minimise an adverse public reaction.

The most desirable setting for kidnappings has been the busy street in an urban area. The prospective kidnappers are able to set up an ambush while attracting minimal attention following such an attack, and the immobilisation of the victim's vehicle, the capture and speedy getaway can be easily and unobtrusively accomplished.

The most dramatic kidnapping form is that which can occur in the context of an airline hijacking. The vast majority of skyjackers seek either to obtain the release of certain political prisoners or to express protest against a particular regime.

Self-appointed avengers can seek retribution through threats or acts of violence, for example the kidnapping of foreign business-men by Latin American terrorists.

Rewards

Kidnapping is demanding, rewarding and lucrative. It requires intricate planning, split-second timing and a large support apparatus to sustain the group holding the victim and to keep security while communicating demands and negotiating with third parties.

▶ Ransoms can be huge, and millions of dollars or pounds can change hands.

▶ Money can be spread under various names in banks in Europe and the USA, from where it can finance more political terrorism.

▶ A kidnapping for ransom can be carried out by a group of any size, criminal or political, ranging from large international organisations to a single cell or even, as in case of children, by a single person.

▶ A decision to kidnap centres on an assessment of the potential victim's family or firm. Are they rich enough to find a large ransom and are they willing to pay?

Kidnappers prefer the ransom to be paid in hard currency in a foreign country in different bank accounts or dumped in cash for collection by accomplices. They may prefer payment in local currency as long as detection is least unlikely.

Volunteers will be needed to drop the money, and negotiators will be in a strong position because the kidnappers will be tense and wish to end the business quickly.

Strengths and weaknesses

The kidnappers' strengths
Holding the initiative is vital. The kidnappers hold the victim and know where everyone on both sides is based. They may be willing to maim their victim while the authorities have self-imposed restraints. The terrorists know that most people will pay rather than allow a husband, child or colleague to be killed.

The kidnappers' weakness
Time is on side of the police, whether measured in days or months. Every extra day brings a greater chance of detection and may accumulate more evidence for arrest and conviction.

Interested parties
The interests of those involved on the side of the law will often conflict. The victim may face conflicts too. His family will probably be less willing to sacrifice his life than he is himself, and his negotiators have a duty to balance their obligations to their client and their obligations, legal or moral, as citizens.

The victim's firm may well be involved. If it is a subsidiary of an overseas corporation, corporate headquarters may see the problem differently from its representatives on the spot.

The police have a dual responsibility – to the victim and to society. In some countries the army can act instead of the police in terrorist operations.

Tutorial

Progress questions

1. Examine the different facts behind the terrorist mindset and account for the different groups that are formed.

2. Is it correct to refer to the unique nature of terrorism strategy?

3. Why are the Irgun Zvai Leumi and the National Liberation Front effective examples of revolutionary groups?

4. How far has terrorism benefited from the growth of technology?

5. Compare and contrast kidnapping and hostage-taking.

Discussion points

1. What do you consider to be the main avenues of terrorist propaganda in a democratic society?

2. What are the main terrorist threats to a free society such as the UK?

3. Why should violence be such a popular option in societies around the world at the present time?

4. Are governments guided in their response to kidnapping and hostage-taking by the identity of the victim?

5. How do you believe governments should try to analyse the inner landscape of terrorism to develop their anti-terrorist legislation?

Practical assignments

1. Produce a character profile of a typical terrorist.

2. Assess the practicalities of adopting either a no ransom or a flexible response approach to hostage situations.

8

The Nature of Revolutionary Violence

One-minute summary – In this chapter we will examine some key themes surrounding the nature of revolutionary violence. In particular we will explore:

▶ the determinants of state terrorism in conflict situations
▶ the determinants of state violence in conflict situations
▶ political violence and the groups which take part
▶ factors in the creation of political violence
▶ the escalation of terroristic violence.

Determinants of state terrorism in conflict situations

Terrorist responses by a state to any challenges are linked to:

▶ the political threat posed by the challengers
▶ the challengers' use of guerrilla and terrorist tactics
▶ the extent of latent popular support for the challengers
▶ the marginal political status of the challengers.

Other issues are the institutionalised terror apparatus, elite access to the maintenance of power through violence, others' successful use of state terror to consolidate power, and the democratic political culture and institutions. There are also concerns of social heterogeneity and stratification and minority elites in highly stratified societies.

It is important to note that the more generalised international and internal political determinants of state violence interact with the direct determinants of state terror to intensify the disposition to rely on terrorist tactics and strategies.

Determinants of state violence in conflict situations

A state considering a violent response to a challenge has to be mindful of:

▶ the weakness or strength of the official
▶ what access the elite has to the maintenance of power by violence
▶ the democratic political culture of its institutions.

From an international perspective it also has to be mindful of:

▶ the external threat
▶ the danger of power wars by proxy
▶ its peripheral international status
▶ the political threat posed by challengers.

All these determinants are linked together by the degree of social heterogeneity and stratification within the state.

Political violence

Factors in the development of political violence

▶ *What* – namely the status, the decision on what type of action to take and the broad objectives to be achieved.

▶ *Who* – leadership is critical and he or she must inspire respect and be able to achieve results. However, a leader needs the members of the organisation to be loyal, cooperative and successful.

▶ *Where* – the domestic/international environment has to be studied to find out levels of support, levels of success, finance and possible repercussions.

▶ *Why* – this depends on the cause and the ideology. One has to be a psychologist (almost) to analyse why events have come to violence, why they take a particular form, and the purpose of the political godfathers behind the violence.

▶ *How* – many factors affect which methods of political violence are used. Strategy is the key, in particular the ability to out-think and out-fight or 'out-bomb' your enemies. Popular support will be in evidence if the strategy works. Organisation is required in terms of cash, equipment, training and target selection. Propaganda and communication have to be leakproof and secure and managed by loyalists and experts. Tactics have to interact with the strategy and both must succeed. Domestic material support can enhance morale and build up patriotic and nationalistic self-confidence. International support is also critical to win the support of like-minded people. Intelligence can be vital to any success, requiring a rapport between groups. Counter-intelligence is also critical, bringing together police, politicians and the military.

Ultimately the key to political violence is knowing when to strike, and what format to adopt – subversion, terrorism, guerrilla warfare or the much feared conventional war using a terrorist or guerrilla base.

Intensity of political violence

Political violence is of many types and varies in intensity. It can be:

▶ *inter-communal* – on behalf of an alleged group interest

▶ *remonstrative* – expressing anger

▶ *praetorian* – aiming to bring about changes through coercion

▶ *repressive* – quelling opposition as a first step in creating a terrorist state

▶ *resistance* – opposing government authority to undermine stability

▶ *terroristic* – the use of murder and destruction, selectively or at random

▶ *revolutionary and counter-revolutionary* – aiming to overthrow an existing political system and replace it with a new regime

▶ *war* – to gain political ends by military victory.

Whatever form it takes, terrorist violence combining any of these forms always involves the use of murder and destruction. Offshoots of such violence can be classed as follows:

▶ *revolutionary terror* – organisational in character

▶ *violence of allegiance* – involving violence and mass support

▶ *functional violence* – the gaining of strategic advantage through specification

▶ *provocative violence* – the exploitation and escalation of a situation to bring about change by violent means

▶ *symbolic violence* – the victim is seen as a figure representative of the enemy.

The creation of political violence

Factors in the creation of political violence are widespread and complex, but above all interrelated, as the table below shows:

What factors	Where factors
Status Action decision Broad objectives	Domestic/international environment Political violence
Who factors	Why factors
Leadership Membership Actors/roles	Cause Ideology
How factors	When factors
Strategy Popular support Organisation Propaganda and communication Tactics Domestic material support International support Intelligence Counter-intelligence	Subversion Terrorism Guerrilla warfare Conventional war

The escalation of terroristic violence

Terrorist violence may be considered to develop through stages classified as follows:

Protest	1 in 10 of the global population
Political extremism	1 in 100
Non-lethal violence	1 in 1000
Killing	1 in 1 million

These four manifestations of violence can include:

► violent demonstrations
► disruption
► sabotage
► robbery
► burning
► bombing
► casual killing
► selective killing and kidnapping.

Maritime terrorism

The escalation described above has even spread onto the high seas. The threats posed to specifically maritime targets are recognised by the International Maritime Organisation which has prepared a Convention for the Suppression of Unlawful Acts against the Safety of Maritime Navigation. This would greatly extend jurisdiction against terrorists launching attacks on ships or offshore platforms, and thus make it easier for police forces to track and arrest them. Air and sea ports and terminals are alive to the possible dangers and their security measures reflect this.

Terrorism, in contrast to routine criminality, calls for special security arrangements because of the political motives of the attackers. In a terrorist attack the authority and sovereignty of the owner of the property is quickly subsumed by governmental agencies. There is a greatly increased risk of death or injury and losses can be far greater. Moreover, insurance repayments and legal support can become confused and complicated.

Tutorial

Progress questions

1. State violence can be instigated by governments and not necessarily by terrorists. Do you agree?

2. Which types of political violence are most effective and why?

3. Under different headings, list as many reasons as you can for the growth of violence.

Discussion point

1. Revolutionary conflict around the world is the greatest challenge in the 21st century. Do you agree? If so, say how and why it has escalated.

Practical assignments

1. Working in groups, consider the chief reasons for state terrorism in conflict situations.

2. Suggest the factors which you deem to be the most important in ending political violence. Look at the issue from the point of view of (a) the police, (b) lawyers, (c) politicians and (d) the military.

3. Consider as many different options as possible as to how terrorist violence escalates and try to provide reasons for why it occurs.

9

The Forces of Counter-Terrorism

One-minute summary – In this chapter the forces of counter-terrorism will be appraised. In particular we will explore:

▶ the role of armies and police forces
▶ measuring government response to terrorism
▶ a 'third force' – pros and cons.

The role of armies and police forces

Their role in countering unconventional warfare

In a liberal democracy any response to terrorism must be acceptable to the government of the day and to the public. Such a response may be undertaken by the army and the police.

Effective police work against terrorism depends on intelligence and intelligence depends on public cooperation. In Britain the government has the power to requisition troops when a threat to order has developed beyond the capacity of the police to deal with it. In any democracy, the army does not act, as a police force does, on behalf of the community as a whole, but on the orders of its political masters to whom it is accountable through its command structure.

There has traditionally been a dichotomy between civil and military relations. Free societies have faced the eternal balancing task of harmonising liberty and national security. Preserving such a balance has been complicated by the fact that the one institution indispensable to the nation's security – the military – exercises a power not necessarily in harmony with an open democratic society.

Mutual understanding in democracies between police and army is improved only by the army's acceptance that there can be no quick solution to troubles which may arise, as has been experienced in Kenya, Cyprus and Northern Ireland.

The army

An army built up in a strong democratic society has a direct idea of its role in countering terrorism, and has to tread the fine line between overreaction and pusillanimity. Modern governments prefer to rely on the police to handle disorder because it reduces the chances of disagreement with the military about their role.

The police

The police are the most appropriate body to maintain internal law and order and the use of armed forces in this role is generally inappropriate.

▶ The police have a special mandate in constitutional theory. They also have the organisation and training to control civil disorder.

▶ There is an overriding necessity for the police to maintain a close relationship with the public.

▶ Because the police operate in the community they are likely to have the necessary intelligence information to enable them to cope with threats to social order.

▶ Because they are seen as a positive force by many sectors of the community, useful information is likely to be forthcoming. An organisation such as the army, lacking normal contact with the community, would find such information difficult to obtain.

▶ If the armed services were to become generally involved in internal peacekeeping, they would have to develop their own intelligence network in the community. This would constitute a major – and to many a threatening – change in civil–military relations which would need considerable justification. It would only be thinkable when the civil police force had lost all hope of maintaining internal order.

The armed forces and internal security

Some people see a legitimate role for the armed services in countering terrorist and other internal security situations. They argue that:

▶ Increased and widespread use of the police would strain resources. In any event police methods are ineffective in this area.

▶ When the social consensus breaks down and social discipline and cohesion are diminished one can expect an upsurge of terrorism and political violence.

▶ The army can quickly rebuild public order by using direct methods.

However, there has to be a balance in the use of the police and the military. Too eager an invocation of military aid to the civil power could easily slip into repression, or at least a serious abuse of civil liberties. On the other hand, too great a concern for democratic sensibilities could well produce a weak response which could lead to the destruction of democracy.

Key aspects of the government response to terrorism

▶ Governments need to clearly define the roles of the police and the armed forces, and where necessary to enact legislation to give effect to their policies in this sphere.

▶ Governments and pressure groups have to analyse their policies in order to evaluate the extent to which they fail to accommodate people's expectations and rights.

▶ In the event of political violence one has to develop a calmer approach as a society rather than look for immediate solutions.

▶ Unfortunately overreaction has characterised government response to terrorism in many parts of the world.

Measuring government response to terrorism

Concessionary policies and the failure to extradite terrorists are associated with an increase in terrorist activity. The establishment of a tough policy following a period of softness appears to require consistent actions applied over a period of time.

A period of soft, concessionary policy may result in the establishment of a terrorist infrastructure. Isolated policy events, regardless of intensity, have no impact when they run counter to general policy implementation. A consistently applied and increasingly tough policy toward incident management is associated with significant decreases in all serious events.

A failure to adopt and implement a tough, consistent incident management policy during a specific period of time can be associated with increases in terrorist activity.

A third force

In an attempt to provide a solution to the issue of whether or not to involve the military in civilian security operations, the creation of a 'third force' or 'paramilitary force' has been mooted by experts. Such a force could either be a significant police unit charged with paramilitary duties or a separate paramilitary organisation. Europe has some of the best examples of such a force:

▶ The Compagnies Républicaines de Sécurité (CRS) is a highly mobile police security force under the control of the French Ministry of the Interior.

▶ The Bereitschaftspolizei (emergency police) and the Bundesgrenzschutz (Federal Border Guard) have a similar role in Germany.

Advantages of a third force
▶ Such an organisation is especially trained to deal with terrorist incidents, and does not have the army role (whose primary mission is external defence) or the police role (whose primary mission is law enforcement/crime prevention).

▶ A third force can be called out at very short notice.

Disadvantages of a third force
▶ It could only be justified by a significant increase in political violence.

▶ More force might be used than necessary.

▶ It could lead to the development of political conflict.

▶ It could be alienated from the public. It would effectively be on call and continuously in training.

Ultimately the idea of a third force goes against the traditions of law and order in many democratic countries.

Tutorial

Progress questions
1. Account for the unease between civil and military relations in government.

2. To what extent should the police deal with anti-terrorism?

3. Would a 'third force' ever be acceptable in the UK?

Discussion points
1. The army can never be a police force (and vice versa) in combating terrorism. Do you agree?

2. What are the public's concerns in the debate about police/army cooperation?

3. Can tensions arise between the police and military in combating terror? If so, what can be done about it?

Practical assignments
1. In a group, some members take the army approach and others the police approach to countering terrorism. From the evidence obtained, in what areas could army/police cooperation become more effective?

2. Discuss practical ways in which government response to terrorism can be measured and made to work.

3. Examine the pros and cons of a 'third force'. Consider as a group whether it would work in the UK.

10

Terrorist Strategy and Tactics

One-minute summary – In this chapter we will examine the operational heart of terrorism, namely its strategy and tactics. In particular we will explore:

▶ terrorist violence and propaganda
▶ the strategy of terrorism
▶ terrorist groups and types of organisations
▶ women and terrorism
▶ international and transnational terrorism
▶ terrorism and the economic threat
▶ current/future issues dictating tactics and strategy.

Terrorist violence and propaganda

Terrorism depends on the degree of violence used and the evil towards which it was directed. The 'issue' raised is enhanced by propaganda, and the violence perpetrated to achieve the goal is organised in great detail.

Defining the types terrorism
Internally, terrorism can produce a reign of terror and state terrorism (vigilantism). Internationally it can cause war and be seen as colonialist or counter-revolutionary. It can also be viewed as a balance of terror.

Directed against the state, internal terrorism can be populist, anarchist or revolutionary. The strength of insurrectional feeling can grow. Internationally it can stand for independence and be directed against the system.

Strategy of terrorism

Terrorism as a philosophy
Terrorism as a coherent philosophy and the kind of terrorism society faces today are new phenomena. Their origins can be traced back to theories of revolutionary warfare developed earlier in the twentieth century. One of the greatest theorists was the Chinese communist leader Mao Tse Tung. Mao developed a coherent theory which integrated what were essentially a set of military tactics used by those who lacked armies. He acknowledged the military basis of political power and emphasised the importance of political power as a substitute for military power. It was considered vital that the guerrillas be highly motivated politically so that, strengthened by the political support of the peasantry, they could survive early military reverses and have the determination to carry out a protracted campaign which would eventually wear down the less committed and dedicated opposition.

Terrorism as violence for effect
The concept of a people's war was not just about arms and resources. It was about how a revolutionary group could eventually defeat militarily superior forces. Terrorism is violence for effect. The actual physical damage it causes is often not important – the aim is to have a dramatic impact on the audience.

Anti-colonial guerrillas after 1945 failed to fully understand the results of their actions, but by placing violent action before an audience they succeeded in neutralising the military muscle of the colonial powers.

Apart from Cuba in 1959, few guerrillas have achieved the success of those colonial freedom fighters:

► Colonial governments were beginning to be viewed as an immoral hangover from history by many citizens of the colonial powers and by influential non-colonial governments.

► Indigenous governments are more unwilling to give up power – that power being all they have – than a colonial government which can give up power in a colony without losing power at home.

From rural to urban guerrilla tactics

The failure of conventional guerrilla tactics against indigenous governments has been particularly obvious in South America where rural guerrillas have failed to advance beyond the remote areas in which they first began fighting. This in turn has led to the development of urban guerrilla tactics which aim to take the struggle directly to the government.

▶ It is in urban guerrilla theory that the tactics of terrorism become most apparent. This theory provides the link between earlier revolutionary theories and modern terrorism.

▶ Urban guerrillas first seek to gain international attention by dramatic acts of violence. Assassinations, bombing, kidnappings, bank robberies and hijacking have all become common weapons for urban political activists.

Other groups have adopted these tactics and carried them further by extending the conflict to individuals and countries not directly involved in the struggle.

Terrorist groups and organisations

Terrorist organisations can be described in a number of ways:

▶ Many have features in common with other organisations and have multiple objectives.

▶ While a terrorist organisation may wish to separate itself from the world (for security, for ideological purity), it has to live within the world. It needs money for weapons and sophisticated equipment.

▶ The need to sustain an income grows as the organisation grows. Terrorist organisations are expensive to maintain.

▶ Terrorist organisations are much like businesses – they exist to generate income and maximise profit. Initially organisations seem to achieve this income through robberies, contributions from supporters and extortion.

▶ As an organisation matures, other sophisticated ways of generating income emerge that are more secure from interference by the security forces or the ebb and flow of operational successes.

▶ It must not be forgotten that people come together to form a terrorist group through a shared sense of ideological purpose.

Psychological forces
Political terrorists are driven to commit acts of violence as a consequence of psychological forces, and individuals are drawn to the path of terrorism in order to commit acts of violence. A great deal may have gone wrong in the lives of people who are drawn to the path of terrorism. There is a high incidence of fragmented families, juvenile crime and failure educationally and vocationally. Terrorists are seen as failure-prone and unable to adapt to societal expectations.

Uniqueness
Each terrorist group is unique and must be studied in the context of its own national culture and history. Nevertheless, the family backgrounds of terrorists do not differ strikingly from the backgrounds of their politically active counterparts. Terrorists do not demonstrate serious psychopathology.

Personality types
Although there is no single personality type, it appears that people who are aggressive and action oriented, and who place greater than normal reliance on the psychological mechanisms of externalisation and splitting, are disproportionately represented among terrorists. Terrorists are especially attractive to like-minded individuals whose credo is 'It's not us – it's them'.

Sense of belonging
For many, membership of the terrorist group may be the first time they truly belonged, the first time they felt truly significant, the

first time they felt that what they did counted. In differentiating between types of terrorist, both the structure of the group and social origin of the members are of consequence. In the autonomous terrorist cell, the leader is within the cell, and cells can be emotional hothouses rife with tension. Group dynamics can vary between nationalist-separatist terrorists and anarchic-ideologues. The former are often known in their communities and maintain relationships with friends and family outside the group, moving into and out of the community with relative ease. In the latter case the decision to cross the boundary and enter the underground illegal group is irrevocable.

Group pressures

Group pressures are magnified for the underground group. The group becomes the only source of information, the only source of confirmation and – in the face of external danger and pursuit – the only source of security.

In any terrorist group, doubts concerning the legitimacy of goals and actions of the group are intolerable. The person who questions a group decision risks the wrath of the group and possible expulsion. Pressures to commit acts of violence are considerable in most groups: individuals become terrorists in order to join terrorist groups and commit acts of terrorism, and indeed justify their existence. Each terrorist group is unique.

The priority of survival

For any group or organisation the highest priority is survival. This is especially true for the terrorist group. To succeed in achieving its espoused cause would threaten the goal of survival. Terrorists whose only sense of significance comes from being terrorists cannot be forced to give up terrorism, for to do so would be to lose their very reason for being. Political terrorism, the product of generational forces, is present for generations to come. There is no short-term solution to the problem of terrorism.

Psychological warfare

Political terrorism is not simply a product of psychological forces. Its central strategy is psychological, for political terrorism, is, at heart, a particularly vicious species of psychological warfare. Until now the terrorists have had a virtual monopoly on the weapon (the television camera), as they manipulate their target audiences through the media. Basically, terrorists perpetuate their organisations by shaping the perceptions of future generations of terrorists.

Examples of terrorist groups

There are many different types of groups in the terrorist world. The list below provides some examples. (Reference can be made to the books in the bibliography for further information.)

▶ *Anarchist* – for example the Angry Brigade in England, active in the late 1960s.

▶ *Separatist* – a separate country for an ethnic group for political reasons, for example the Basque separatist organisation in Spain, Euzkadi Ta Askatasuna (ETA).

▶ *Ultra-left* – for example the Baader Meinhof Gang, one of the oldest and most brutal of the terrorist organisations in Germany, aiming for an armed anti-imperialist struggle.

▶ *Latin guerrillas* – for example, the Montoneros in Argentina, a group of urban guerrillas wishing to take over a regime.

▶ *Criminal gangs* – for example the Mafia criminal organisation engaged in bombing, kidnapping and assassinations.

▶ *Secessionist groups* – for example the Irish Republican Army, an illegal military organisation, with links to Sinn Fein and the longest-lived terrorist organisation in history, exhibiting a remarkable continuity in both goal and method.

▶ *Cover names* – for example Black September, a hard line Palestinian group opposed to a political settlement and preferring to commit individual acts of violence.

▶ *Pathological* – for example the Weathermen in the USA, a group committing domestic violence on behalf of minorities allegedly discriminated against.

▶ *Marxist revolutionary* – for example the Brigate Rosse, Italian urban guerrillas attacking the 'enemies of the working class'.

▶ *Sects/secret societies* – for example the Neo-Nazis, German right-wing extremists involved in violence against the state.

▶ *Minorities in insurgencies* – there are many examples, of which the Kurds in Iraq are the most active, demanding concessions from the regimes and interspersing violence with limited conciliation, yet factionalised into two groups.

Women and terrorism

Many traditional observers would find the idea of women terrorist groups a contradiction in terms. However, in certain guerrilla and terrorist groups, such as the Tupamaros in Uruquay, the Montoneros in Argentina and some of the Japanese groups, women act as collectors of intelligence, take part in operations as couriers, nurses and medical personnel and maintain safe houses for weapons, funds and supplies.

Leftist groups tend to be exceptions and sometimes have female leaders. For example, Leila Khaled and Fusako Shigenobu were leaders of the Popular Front for the Liberation of Palestine and the Japanese Red Army respectively.

Most female terrorists act in a supportive capacity. They play a useful role because a group of women together are less visible than a group of men. In the Baader Meinhof terrorist group in West Germany in the 1970s and 1980s, women formed a third of the operational personnel and took part in robberies, burglaries and kidnappings.

Unmarried women terrorists are the rule, except in the Tupamaros. Women usually work in a familiar or specific area, with many having an urban background.

There is a general lowering of the entry age into operational activity and some women have been operationally trained and adopt key leadership roles. Many women have the nomadic lifestyle of the groups and have a desire for action and money.

Terrorism in the late twentieth century has been an 'equal opportunity employer'. Recent observations have shown that female members of terrorist groups have proved to be tougher, more fanatical and more loyal. They also possess a greater capacity for suffering. Women have, in some terrorist groups, tended to remain members longer than men, on the average. Women are more than willing today to do the unthinkable, such as carrying suitcases loaded with explosive onto airplanes.

International and transnational terrorism

International terror and transnational terror appear similar, but actually have different meanings:

▶ *international terror* – means attacks against foreign citizens or targets within or beyond the frontiers of the terrorists' own state.

▶ *transnational terror* – is undertaken by autonomous non-state actors, with groups operating outside the frontiers of their home country.

International terrorism
International terrorism, marks a new departure in the tactics of terror.

▶ It is the newest branch in the evolution of modern revolutionary and guerrilla warfare theories.

▶ It elevates individual acts of violence to the level of strategy.

▶ It denigrates conventional military power by substituting dramatic violence played out for the people watching.

▶ It violates the conventional rules of engagement – it encompasses innocent bystanders.

▶ It makes the world its battlefield – it recognises no boundaries to the conflict, no neutral nations.

The views of proponents of revolutionary warfare
The most prominent proponents of revolutionary warfare, such as

Regis Debray, argue that terrorism has a limited and secondary role only to revolutionary warfare. It must be employed selectively and cautiously or the tactic may backfire.

Carlos Marighela, the guerrilla theorist, believed urban operations to be secondary to rural ones. To him, urban guerrilla warfare was meant to wear out, demoralise and distract the enemy forces. In this way it permitted the emergence and survival of rural guerrilla warfare which is destined to play a decisive role in the revolutionary war. Marighela advocated terrorism as a tactic to provoke repression, but also warned against the use of terrorism as an end in itself.

The need for popular support
Revolutionary warfare requires the commitment and cooperation of the populace. It is not possible to obtain such commitment in the long term if the populace suffers under a campaign of terror. The collapse of the Malayan communist insurgency (1948–54) can be partially attributed to the insurgents' excessive use of terrorism. Such a collapse will follow the indiscriminate use of terrorism against the general population.

The trend to nihilism
While some groups do adhere to the theoretical propositions of revolutionary warfare, there is increasing evidence of a trend towards nihilistic tendencies in some terrorist groups. They have no theoretical or tactical limits to their behaviour. They are not concerned to win the 'hearts and minds' of the people, but rather seek only to destroy. With the possibilities for mass destruction or mass disruption which exist in modern society, such groups present a danger and challenge that has never existed in the history of terrorism to date. It is against these groups that society will have to put its best skills in the future.

The dangers of international terrorism
▶ States can develop 'proxy' terror as a weapon of coercive diplomacy against rival states.

▶ Sophisticated weaponry can be acquired and used.

▶ There is an increasing number of international terrorist

operations and a development in bilateral and multilateral cooperation between them.

▶ Local power balances can be disrupted.

In addition to these danger factors, a number of developments may lead to increased terrorist activities over the long term, including:

▶ a rebirth of racism and growth of membership in racist groups

▶ a resurgence of religious fanaticism that results in the proliferation of cults

▶ growing contempt for the criminal justice system

▶ an increase in single-issue policies and in the number of narrow-interest groups

▶ an unmeasured decline in police intelligence activities

▶ growing mistrust of government and corporations as incompetent, negligent and irresponsible in protecting public health and safety

▶ a sense of insecurity as a result of a growing perception that law enforcement cannot effectively protect citizens.

Shift to transnational terror

Transnational terrorism is carried out by basically autonomous non-state actors whether or not they enjoy some degree of support from sympathetic states. It has grown because of:

▶ the regular failure of revolutionary campaigns in the Third World

▶ the repeated collapse of other new strategies

▶ the recognition of a potential for exploiting the mass media

▶ political trends in the Third World.

Terrorism and the economic threat

Terrorist threats can be expensive. Aspects to consider are:

▶ the levels and kind of victimisation

▶ the costs of terror

▶ corporate, governmental and intergovernmental attitudes

▶ relations between corporate security and law enforcement agencies

▶ current needs and future prospects for developing a national anti-terror managerial system.

Current and future issues of tactics and strategy

The terrorist potential

The potential for terrorist violence in the future is multifarious. Major international sporting events, royalty and heads of state remain vulnerable.

Many people feel powerless in the face of growing federal trading blocs such as the European Union and the North America Free Trade Association. Frustration can boil over into bomb threats, abduction and kidnapping as a means of exerting international pressure.

Multinational companies can be threatened in similar ways. The threats may emanate from the unemployed and young people disaffected within the system. This in turn can be exploited by the Mafia and organised crime in many more transnational situations than before. More secessionist violence will occur around the world as minorities become more and more disaffected.

Chemical and biological warfare

Terrorism will employ chemical and biological warfare coupled with the exploitation the media and its psychological effects. Among other things anti-chemical and biological warfare will necessitate development of immediate detection and neutralisation units. These are now non-existent. The trend of placing explosives in public places to be detonated from a distance by sophisticated systems will continue. Car bombs and suicide killings will feature within the fundamentalist religious organisations.

The need for an international response

Terrorism changes its character from one country to another, from one target to another and from one social environment to another. No country in the world is immune to this threat. Thus perhaps there needs to be an international body to fight terrorism, a body with full legal status and recognition, a budget and operative authority. It would need to eradicate international terrorism, deal with the economic and legal aspects of anti-terrorism activity and institutionalise the international transfer of intelligence. Experts in anti-terror warfare qualified in effective combat against terrorism have to be supported by national governments and international organisations.

Moslem fundamentalism

Currently the spread of fundamentalism remains a cause of growing concern. If the North African nations were to become a front line in the war against fundamentalism, there would be grave implications in terms of security for Europe arising from the increased militarisation of the area.

Algeria exemplifies such worries. A very fluid society, Algeria is balanced precariously between Islam and the West and has been wracked by the activities of two militant groups resulting in at least 60,000 deaths since 1992. Here the terrorist capacity to cause mayhem continues undiminished. At the other end of the Middle East in Iran there are currently 17 organisations in Teheran that are directly involved in one form of terrorism or another, most of it abroad. Thousands of Iranians and many foreigners have 'graduated' from terrorist training camps in the country. The victory by a moderate in the presidential election in Iran has caused Western optimism. Whether this optimism is justified or misplaced, remains to be seen.

The difficulty of finding a solution

Many conflicts of a terrorist nature remain hard to solve, whether those conflicts involve drugs, minorities with severe grievances, or the irrationality of the protagonists in terms of their motivation. On the part of security forces and governments, dilemmas are developing on how to deal with terrorism. Terrorism is constantly changing in terms of violence, the geographical extent of operations, the intended outcome and, above all, the bizarre characters of the participants. The horrors of cyberterrorism still remain in their infancy.

The response of governments

Primarily one has to ask whether the fundamental causes of terrorism are being addressed by governments. The question of when a government itself becomes the terrorist is a moot point. Some governments can have ulterior motives: treating terrorists as common criminals may be part of a strategy to conceal the existence of social conflict. If governments face high levels of social conflict they can avoid mention of the terrorist label. On the other hand, governments enjoying a high level of consensus may publicly condemn terrorism but allow discussion of terrorist ideology and motives.

Governments which see themselves as guardians of order in international relations can maximise the terrorist menace for their own domestic audience, just as in the post-1945 period the Soviet threat and communist challenge was emphasised by the West.

Nevertheless in the face of a growing and changing terrorist threat, leaders must have the courage to do what is required even in the face of the most stinging criticism. Legally constituted governments like to think they are characterised by formal legitimacy and behaviour as opposed to the formless illegitimacy of terrorists. Often, counter-terrorism's shoot-to-kill policy, its abrogation of due process and its frequent resort to torture give credence to the observation that a government's ethical norms may be abandoned. Counter-terrorism policies may increasingly have to co-opt terrorist strategy to be seen to be successful in the war against terrorism.

Terrorism in many ways has become emblematic of the times in which we live. It can almost be built into a cult by the media. Far from going away, the terrorism of autonomous groups is harder to deal with. They have no protector to lean on, no vital interests other than their own cause or lives to be threatened. Some have goals so utopian that no compromise exists that could entice them to cease fire.

Even in the New World Order the terrorism debate remains vague and complex. After the moral outrage at indiscriminate killing and wounding, there remains uncertainty as to what to do about it. The powers of anti-terrorism adopted by many democratic governments is seen as undermining civil liberties which raises increasing doubts in people's minds as to their efficacy.

The extreme right in the USA

In the USA the greatest immediate threat from terrorist groups was formerly seen to come from violent fringes of the extreme right. The activities of this section of society are strewn with religious symbolism and are inherently anti-federal. Among the Christian right there is fear of a single-world government, a single universal currency, a cashless society and the increasingly sophisticated technological capability of government to monitor the religious activities of citizens. Such fear is becoming an excuse for violence among millennial groups in the USA. Unlike the violent extremists of the left in the 1970s and 1980s who decided to go underground, the violent extremists of the right are perfecting strategies to maintain an above-ground presence for recruiting purposes while developing an underground cellular network.

In the USA as elsewhere one of the worst aspects of terrorism is its fearful images that tend to lack discrimination and careful definition. Little resistance is offered to inflated claims, undocumented allegations and the suppression of facts. Moreover, if the threat of terrorism is greater today than it has ever been, then one must ask whether the capacities to respond are adequate. Are governments able to identify the threats and mobilise counter-terrorist resources? Terrorist attacks by smaller and smaller groups are more and more possible in the future and, given technological sophistication, more and more probable.

There is substantial evidence to show that religious fanatics will prove more deadly than past terrorists because it is much harder to infiltrate groups with no systematic organisation. Many states will have to upgrade their counter-terrorist strategies to guard against those that would welcome Armageddon. Thus there is a greater sense of urgency towards a coordinated international legislative approach to twenty-first century terrorism.

Technology and the Internet

From a technological point of view the outlook is particularly bleak. As powerful computers become less costly, easier to obtain, and simple to use, cyberspace crime, like terrorism, will become more common and open to all. The Internet enables all kinds of extremist groups to propagate their messages in ways never before dreamed possible. Even more frightening is the possibility that self-imposed constraints against using nuclear weapons seem to be breaking down and weapons-grade nuclear material and nuclear weapons are more accessible than before. Beyond profit and religion the new motives for terrorism could include the desire for fun or entertainment, or simply the challenge. Society will need to counter one of the major motives emerging for terrorism – the pure quest for attention.

Tutorial

Progress questions

1. Do terrorists and revolutionaries have any legitimate 'issues'?

2. How far is political terrorism's central strategy psychological?

3. It is said that women are more extreme and more loyal when involved in a revolutionary situation. Do you agree?

4. How can revolutionary activity affect a country's economy?

Discussion points

1. Is there any value in trying to classify terrorist groups when so many terrorist actions are characteristic of more than one group?

2. Which is more dangerous: international or transnational terrorism?

3. Would you differentiate between tactics and strategy when considering developments in terrorist warfare?

Practical assignments

1. What typology of terrorism do you agree with, and why?

2. Working in groups, look collectively at the roles of different terrorist groups. Which do you think could possibly cooperate with governments to end violence?

3. Research as many definitions as possible of international and transnational terrorism and summarise which could be workable on the part of governments to curb the violence. Why can't international and transnational terrorism be united into a workable definition?

11

Future Developments in Terrorism

One-minute summary – In this chapter one will examine the possible future development of terrorism. In particular we will explore:

▶ chemical and biological terrorism
▶ nuclear terror
▶ international terrorism and technological developments
▶ terrorism and the New World Order
▶ narco-terrorism
▶ new terrorism in the twenty-first century
▶ unanswered questions about terrorism and revolutionary warfare.

Chemical and biological terrorism

Chemical weapons such as nerve agents constitute substantially greater threats than nuclear bombs, being capable of producing hundreds of thousands of fatalities. A small thermonuclear weapon might produce 100,000 casualties, but biological agents – both toxins and living organisms – create the possibility of several millions of casualties in a single incident.

Types of chemical and biological weapons
Some examples of chemical and biological weapons are:

▶ *Organophosphates* – these so-called nerve agents can be synthesised by a moderately competent chemist with limited laboratory facilities. Indeed, for some terrorist groups lacking a chemist and laboratory, some forms of these agents are available commercially as insecticides.

▶ *Botulinal toxin* – this is a highly toxic nerve agent found in spoiled or ill-prepared food.

▶ *Anthrax* – this is 100,000 times more effective as an agent of destruction than the highly toxic nerve gas similar to that used in Japan by a religious cult.

Many chemical and biological agents are readily produced or may often be obtained through legitimate sources.

Problems in use

Few groups have yet used such weapons. The reasons include:

▶ It is difficult to disseminate the toxic substances in sufficient quantities.

▶ There are technical problems in using such a weapon as a bargaining chip (aside from the technical problems of constructing the device).

▶ There are problems over what demands could be made. Any 'rational' terrorist group would be unlikely to waste the potential leverage afforded by 'going biological/nuclear' merely to effect the release of prisoners or demand a ransom.

▶ The problem is one of the fulcrum of bargaining power. If the terrorists are unwilling to dismantle the threat by surrendering the device, governments are less likely to yield.

▶ If the terrorists surrender the device, how do they enforce their demands, particularly if these are for such things as changes in policy?

However, one cannot be complacent about the terrorist threat of nuclear, biological and chemical weapons. At the time of writing, the USA is under sustained attack by an unknown group. Anthrax spores are being sent through the postal system, some people have been infected and there have been deaths.

The Tokyo attack

A deadly nerve gas was released in an attack on the Tokyo underground in 1995. This was a new threat, posed by a mass religious movement motivated by a mystical, almost transcendental and divinely inspired imperative. Its use suggests that the constraints (both self-imposed and technical) which previously inhibited the terrorist use of weapons of mass destruction are breaking down. The nature of religious and quasi-religious terrorists – as compared with their secular counterparts – suggests that the former terrorists will be among the most likely of the potential categories of non-state perpetrators to use such weapons.

However, like many people, terrorists themselves appear to fear such powerful contaminants and toxins about which they know little and which they are uncertain how to fabricate and safely handle, much less effectively deploy and dispense.

Despite this, the event in 1995 clearly demonstrated that it is possible for terrorists to execute a successful chemical attack, and may conceivably have raised the stakes for terrorists elsewhere.

Nuclear terror

The issue of nuclear power and nuclear weapons has itself provoked violence. Anti-nuclear activists could conceivably detonate a nuclear weapon to illustrate their contention that such weapons must be banned. So far no such incident has happened, but the growing debate about the subject makes the prospect uncomfortably easy to imagine.

The threat

Advanced technology and the materials required to construct a nuclear weapon are available to terrorists today. The devices may be difficult to manufacture, but its not impossible to do so. They could also be stolen, purchased or supplied by supporting states. The sabotage or takeover of a nuclear facility is also feasible and would be a far cheaper option for the terrorists.

International terrorism and technological developments

Contemporary international terrorism reflects a number of recent technological developments which have enhanced the use of terrorist tactics:

▶ Modern air travel provides unprecedented worldwide mobility.

▶ Radio, television and communication satellites provide instantaneous access to a worldwide audience.

▶ Weapons and explosives have become increasingly available to anybody with the money to buy them.

▶ Modern society presents new areas of vulnerability, for example air travel.

Drugs and terrorism – narco-terrorism

Narco-terrorism is the networking of the trade in illicit drugs and terrorism. It links the two most feared and destructive forces plaguing modern society – terror and drugs.

The drug trade offers vast profits for nations which, although they want to continue to sponsor terrorist groups, find their coffers seriously depleted. The use of drugs to underwrite the costs of terrorism adds a new dimension to law enforcement efforts to combat both drugs and terrorism. Both Syria and Iran have engaged in international drug smuggling to help finance their support for terrorist groups.

The main players
The underworld of narco-terrorism has three main players:

▶ Terrorist groups such as the Tamils, the Basque separatists and some Sikh extremists.

▶ The government officials and intelligence services of nations such as Iran and Cuba whose foreign policy includes the exporting of revolution, and the criminals dealing in narcotics who dispense political violence and terror.

▶ Through a network of contacts, narco-terrorists deal in weapons, launder money, share intelligence information, trade false passports, share safe havens and offer other forms of assistance.

There is a loose global alliance of two elements of the criminal world: those who deal in drugs have long become inured to dealing in death, and find little difference in their relationship with terrorists.

Example
Lebanon remains a primary source of hashish for the international market, and both production and trafficking occur either with the permission or with the collusion of a number of terrorist organisations and Syrian military officers in the occupying forces. Nearly all of the militant groups in the area obtain revenue from the drug industry, either directly or by 'protecting' the contraband as it is transported through their area of influence. The 'industry' generates an estimated $1 billion per year, most of which is used to finance the activities of terrorist groups and sponsoring states.

It has been said that drugs could destroy the western world. Is the unholy triangle of drug traffickers, terrorists and state officials really committed to the destruction of the western world? Or is it just a mischance? Either way, we should try to bring about cooperation between the agencies charged with combating drugs and those pledged to combating terrorism.

Escalation of terrorism

There are several factors which help explain the escalation of terrorism:

1. Like soldiers in a war, terrorists who have been in the field for many years have been brutalised by the long struggle. Killing becomes easier.

2. As terrorism has become more commonplace, the public has become to a degree desensitised. Terrorists can no longer obtain the same amount of publicity using the same tactics they used ten years ago or more. They may feel compelled to

escalate their violence in order to retain public attention, or to make an impact on governments which have become more resistant to their demands.

3. Terrorists have become technically more proficient, enabling them to operate on a higher level of violence.

4. The composition of some terrorist groups has changed as the faint-hearted who have no stomach for indiscriminate killing drop out or are ejected by more ruthless elements.

5. The religious nature of current conflicts, as in the Middle East, tends toward mass murder. As we have seen throughout history, presumed 'divine approval' for the killing of pagans, heathens or infidels can permit acts of great destruction and self-destruction.

6. Finally, state sponsorship has provided terrorists with the resources and technical know-how to operate at a higher or more lethal level of violence.

Terrorism and the New World Order

Terrorist violence can be committed both by states and sub-state organisations. The activity becomes international terrorism when the citizens of more than one country are involved; it is internal terrorism when confined within the borders of single states.

A democratic response
A democratic response to terrorism has to comprise:

▶ No surrender to the terrorists.

▶ No deals and no concessions despite blackmail and intimidation.

▶ The desire to bring terrorists to justice by prosecution and conviction before courts of law.

▶ Firm measures to penalise state sponsors who give terrorists safe haven, weapons, explosives, cash, and moral and diplomatic support.

▶ A determination never to allow terrorist intimidation to block or derail political and diplomatic efforts to resolve conflicts in war-torn regions.

Security experts have become alarmed that since the dismantling of the then EC's internal frontiers in 1992 there has been evidence that terrorists and organised criminal gangs such as the Mafia have been taking full advantage of the new political architecture in Europe.

Terrorists can exploit the freedoms of an open and democratic society to mount attacks. On the other hand, the very legitimacy of democracy in the eyes of its citizens provides a kind of inner moral strength which helps the system to withstand attempts to subvert or overthrow it. However, as long as tyrannies exist, terrorists will find sponsorship support, succour and safe haven.

The new terrorism in the twenty-first century

The diminishing ranks of state-sponsored terrorists in the twentieth century are being replaced in the new millennium by 'freelance' extremist groups which are supported outside national boundaries. Given technological sophistication terrorist attacks are probable, especially by small, radical dissident groups. The rage of fundamentalists is unrestrained and as a result democracy is under growing threat.

Patriot terrorism

Patriot terrorism, more than any other form, has brought terrorist violence to the United States. The patriot subculture has its own literature and rhetoric. It is characterised by identity theology, technology, the availability of the tools of violence, the terrorist acts of their cohorts, offensive acts committed by their perceived enemies and fears over the coming millennium. Many of their acts are committed by small, autonomous, leaderless resistance cells or lone offenders.

Violence is directed against government targets, such as the federal building in Oklahoma City in 1995, the World Trade Centre in 2001, and will continue this way. Credit for many of the attacks will not be claimed by the perpetrators. Instead they will invoke the strategy called 'propaganda of the deed' whereby the target itself indicates the motive. Such targets include media outlets, financial institutions, abortion clinics, international gay establishments and civil rights groups.

Throughout the world's impoverished societies there is a call to religious fanaticism. Compounding the problem is the fact that many of these religious zealots are freelancers who take it upon themselves to commit acts of terrorism in the name of the deity. Tracking them is difficult because they do not necessarily align themselves with any specific group. Those that do, join together in loose configurations giving little away to law enforcement authorities.

Cyber-terrorism is an entirely new phenomenon brought into being as computers have become cheaper, smaller and more user-friendly. Attacking high-tech crime with high-tech crime-fighting is, in the long run, counter-productive. The level of state secrecy and public surveillance necessary to accomplish even a semblance of safety from terrorists in society will only replace one source of terror with another.

The creation of the internet and the world wide web has been referred to as the beginning of the information revolution. Information provided by the Internet may be used to stimulate or legitimate terrorist activity. It is certain that the Internet in general and the world wide web will come to play a key role in understanding protest groups and how they function in society.

The willingness of terrorists to engage in acts of mass destruction has increased. Self-imposed constraints still exist, but they seem to be breaking down as the motives that lead to armed conflict change. At some point in the future the opportunity and capacity for serious nuclear terrorism could reach those willing to take advantage of it.

Millenarianism

Personal redemption through violent means is a millenarian theme found in many terrorist belief systems. Violence is often viewed as essential to the coming of the millennium. Believers may be willing to violate the rules of the old order in an effort to bring in the new order – often conceived of in terms of total liberation. Restraints are abandoned and the terrorist is wrapped in an impenetrable cloak of belief in the absolute righteousness of his cause and the certainty of ultimate success.

If all violence brings the new order closer, then no violence – regardless of its consequences – can be regarded as a failure. The terrorist always 'wins' in this struggle. Twenty-first century movements have varied in tone from the most violent aggression to the mildest pacifism, and from the most ethereal spirituality to the most earth-bound materialism.

Millenarianism is both a modern and a worldwide phenomenon. Terrorism, in the twenty-first century will:

▶ certainly continue, both in relation to weapons and tactics

▶ probably increase

▶ be characterised by more large-scale incidents

▶ will enter the world of high technology and mass destruction, with huge loss of life as witnessed on 11 September 2001 in New York and Washington

▶ continue to be exploited by states for their own purposes

▶ increase the chance of a protracted worldwide guerrilla war

▶ create crises, forcing governments and corporations to divert more resources toward combating them.

The targets of terrorism
The future targets of terrorism will be much the same as today:

▶ the representatives of governments and the symbols of nations – notably diplomats and airlines

▶ the representatives of economic systems – e.g. corporations and corporate executives

▶ the symbols of policies and presence – e.g. military officials

▶ political or other leaders.

Unanswered questions on terrorism

There are many unanswered questions on the phenomenon of terrorism and revolutionary warfare. The following should pose a challenge to any interested reader.

1. How would it help society to identify a common terrorist psychosis, personality or mindset?

2. Can we talk of a typical terrorist at all, or is the term too imprecise, too slippery?

3. How does a person become a terrorist?

4. What are the current theories regarding terrorist behaviour?

5. Are terrorist bombers and hijackers more like their non-political criminal counterparts, or are terrorist bombers more like terrorist hijackers and other terrorists?

6. What are the principal elements of a terrorist group's modus operandi?

7. How does the level of violence relate to a terrorist group's cultural background?

8. What factors are considered by a terrorist group in planning and executing an operation?

9. How does the decision-making process vary from group to group?

10. How do terrorists measure success – both the success of an individual operation as well as progress toward their perceived long-term goals?

11. Is extensive press coverage of a terrorist operation in itself a sufficient payoff if other results or concessions are not achieved?

12. If terrorists become disillusioned, do they escalate or simply vow to struggle on in the same way for decades if necessary?

Tutorial

Progress questions

1. Discuss whether the threat of chemical/biological terrorism is overplayed?

2. Why was the attack in Japan involving sarin a turning point in the lethal nature of terrorism?

3. Narco-terrorism is basically the most uncontrollable form of terrorism. Is this correct?

4. Do you believe there are peaks and troughs in the progress of terrorism, or is there a consistent escalation?

5. Should millenarianism be viewed as an American phenomenon or should the outside world be more concerned?

Discussion points

1. Which explanation for the escalation of terrorism do you believe is the most convincing?

2. What do you understand by millennial terrorism?

3. Do you think terrorism, guerrilla warfare and revolutionary warfare will play a trend-setting role in the new century? Give your reasons.

4. Why are there so many unanswered questions on terrorism?

Practical assignments

1. Consider which areas of terrorist violence are likely develop to in future years. Build some projections taking account of some of the current extreme possibilities such as chemical and nuclear terror.

2. Draw up an action plan for governments to follow in combating the new terrorism in the new century.

3. Critically appraise the links in domestic and foreign policy of any democratic country in its effort to combat narco-terrorism.

12

Illustrations of Aspects of Terrorism

One-minute summary – In this chapter will we look at various case studies and other scenarios which have been chosen to provide a broad cross-section of the issues in terrorist and revolutionary conflict. In particular we will explore:

▶ tactics and strategy
▶ the Red Brigades (Brigate Rosse)
▶ the *Achille Lauro* affair of 1985
▶ the elements of the terrorist act
▶ ideology and terrorism
▶ Abu Nidal
▶ terrorism as an accepted method of future warfare
▶ the international development of terrorism
▶ the kidnapping of James Cross in Quebec 1970
▶ international humanitarian law and the rights of terrorists
▶ counter-terrorism
▶ terrorism, intelligence and the law
▶ crisis and risk management
▶ future trends.

Tactics and strategy

Various tactics and strategies have been adopted by terrorists and guerrilla fighters, and those pursuing revolutionary war. Such people have one trait in common: they live in the future, they live for that distant – yet to them attainable – point in time when they will assuredly triumph over their enemies and realise their ultimate political destiny.

The art of managing the armed men under their control and the skilful techniques adopted as a result, terrorists are without

equal. They can impose upon their enemy the place, time and
conditions for fighting preferred by themselves – as events in places
as far apart geographically as Northern Ireland, Mozambique,
Myanmar and Colombia have shown. Points for consideration
when examining terrorist tactics and strategy include:

► terrorist and guerrilla groups
► political violence induced by terrorists
► differentiation between terrorists and guerrillas
► types of terrorist groups
► violence – political and terrorist
► the exploitation of fear
► the factors behind terrorist thinking
► the current situation regarding terrorism and guerrilla
  activity
► colonialist struggles – Palestine and Algeria
► terrorism and its development as a strategy – its origins in
  revolutionary warfare, Maoist thought
► the concept of a people's war the role of anti-colonial
  guerrillas
► urban guerrillas – leading to international terrorism
► revolutionary warfare thinkers, e.g. Debray
► Modern terrorist mindsets: left-wing groups, ethno-
  nationalist/separatist groups, right-wing groups and religious
  fanatics
► the unique nature of terrorism strategy.

The Red Brigades (Brigate Rosse)

This organisation of Marxist-Leninist urban guerrillas was
established in 1969, initially to attack industrialists, the 'enemy
of the working class'. It was particularly active in the industrial
centres of Northern Italy, where kidnapping operations were a
regular occurrence, in order to achieve large-scale ransom
payments. For the past decade the group has operated in most
parts of the country, intimidating, wounding or murdering. The
Brigades have always hoped to create a situation in which a fascist
coup could be provoked, leading to a return of the Communist

Party of Italy to a revolutionary role which the Party had abandoned by cooperation with the government.

The Brigades compare their activity to the work of the Provisional IRA, the Red Army Faction (Baader Meinhof Group) in West Germany and the Palestine Liberation Organisation. In 1981 these links were borne out in the call for the creation of a terrorist international in which the central role would be played by the Brigades and the Red Army Faction. Support roles could be fulfilled by the European revolutionary forces of ETA in Spain and the IRA, once they had abandoned nationalism.

After two or three years of increasingly violent acts, police arrested Renato Curcio and Alberto Franceschini, the chief ideologues of the Brigades. Both were given prison sentences; Curcio was then sprung from jail, rearrested and returned to jail, despite threats of further activity by the terrorists if Curcio was put in jail. The trial was suspended.

Aldo Moro

The greatest success for the Red Brigades was in March 1978, when members seized Aldo Moro, the president of the Christian Democratic Party. Moro had been Prime Minister on a number of occasions between 1963 and 1976. He was threatened with trial by a people's court, and the release of certain detainees was demanded as the price of freeing their hostage. No concessions were made by the government, and in April the Brigades declared that Moro had been found guilty and the death sentence passed on him at the 'people's court'. In May he was shot dead and his body dumped in the boot of a car in the centre of Rome. Within weeks nine terrorists were arrested and charged with complicity in the murder.

Meanwhile, the trial of Curcio continued and in June he was sentenced to 15 years in prison for forming an armed group to subvert the state and for carrying out political kidnappings. In February 1979 he was given a further 12-year prison sentence for attempted murder and possession of arms, and a six-year sentence in November for his escape from prison in 1975, while nine other Brigades members were also sentenced to up to six years in prison for 'terrorist activities'. Finally, in October 1979, Curcio received a further ten-year sentence, and 13 other Brigades members were given up to ten years for insulting the judges and inciting Brigades followers to insurrection during the 1978 trial.

James Dozier

The killings and kidnappings continued, ranging from police, magistrates and directors to civil servants, councillors, journalists and armed services personnel. In this latter category was Brigadier-General James Dozier, a US Army staff officer and deputy commander of NATO land forces in Southern Europe. Dozier was abducted in Verona in December 1981. He was tried by a people's court, found guilty and threatened with death. However, in late January 1982 police acting on information received from a suspect freed Dozier unhurt and arrested five Brigades members who were holding him in an apartment in Padua. This was the first time Italian police had succeeded in freeing a hostage seized by the Brigades. Later, the court passed prison sentences totalling over 300 years on the defendants.

The aftermath of the Dozier kidnap produced considerable success for the security forces and many persons were arrested on terrorism charges from the Brigades and affiliated organisations. Many arms caches and safe houses also were found. Most of these terrorists realised that they had failed to attain their political aims. Indeed, some of the Dozier abductors issued an appeal to fellow members of the Brigades to give up the armed struggle, which they claimed had proved a failure over the previous decade. A bloodstained struggle could produce no change in the political programme.

By January 1983 the last of the Moro kidnappers was sentenced, and out of 63 defendants, life sentences were passed on 32 of them for 17 murders (including that of Moro), 11 attempted murders and 4 kidnappings between 1977 and 1980. In 1980 the Brigades had an estimated membership of about 500 activists, with a further 10,000 supporters. Thereafter the active membership declined, principally because of the success of the security authorities in penetrating and neutralising the organisation's cells in different parts of the country.

The *Achille Lauro*

The Italian cruise liner *Achille Lauro* was hijacked on 7 October 1985 in Egyptian waters by members of the Tunis-based faction of the Palestine Liberation Front (an arm of the Palestine Liberation Organisation). The guerrillas demanded the release of 50 Palestinian prisoners and murdered a disabled Jewish American. The Egyptian government called in a negotiator, Abu Abbas, who promised the guerrillas safe passage if they released the ship.

However, US intelligence sources were organising their own response. The Egyptian plane on which the guerrillas were being taken out of Egypt was ambushed by US war planes and forced to land in Italy where the hijackers were taken into custody by the Italian government.

The issue raised interesting points. Was it wrong of Egypt to allow the hijackers into port and then to assist them in leaving the country? Was the USA justified in its actions against the hijackers or was it guilty of state terrorism? How far are 'rights' to commit acts of terror and violence derived from 'wrongs'?

Elements of the terrorist act

The terrorist act has four chief aspects: there is an act of violence; it is undertaken against innocent persons; there is a political motive; and it exposes ordinary people to fear and terror. This should help to clarify whether the following were terrorist acts

► *The Oklahoma bombing* – In April 1995 a federal building in Oklahoma was blown apart by a car/truck bomb planted by the Militias movement. Over 160 people were killed. Such direct action was taken by paramilitaries against what they saw as intrusion by the federal government. The incident caused general panic and major repercussions.

► *Archbishop Romero* – On 24 March 1980 in El Salvador, Archbishop Oscar Romero prepared for mass in the main cathedral of the capital San Salvador. He was a frequent critic of the government and the day before he had tried to persuade the military to disarm and stop attacking the peasantry. As he prepared to serve the Eucharist the priest was murdered. Many believed that the orders for his death came from the highest level of the El Salvadorian government.

▶ *Geoffrey Jackson* – In January 1971 the Uruguayan guerrilla group the Tupamaros kidnapped Geoffrey Jackson, the British ambassador, and held him in a basement for eight months. The British government refused to pay a ransom. Jackson was eventually released as a gesture of goodwill, as the group was desperate to win working-class support and wished to show the world that they did not murder all their victims.

Ideology and terrorism

To pursue their ideology and right to self-determination, terrorists commit violence. Consider whether any of the following were acts of terror and for what cause were they committed and whether anyone saw justification.

▶ *Assassination of Yitzak Rabin* – In November 1995 Rabin, the Israeli Prime Minister, was gunned down by a young Jewish extremist who believed he had sold out to the Palestinians. The assassin wished to derail the withdrawal of Israel from the occupied territories on the West Bank.

▶ *Assassination of Indira Gandhi* – In October 1984 the Prime Minister of India, Indira Gandhi, was murdered by her Sikh bodyguards in the garden of her New Delhi home. Her murder was an act of revenge for Operation Blue Star, the storming of the Sikhs' holiest shrine at Amritsar in June 1984. The Sikhs viewed this as an act of desecration.

▶ *The bombing of Tripoli in 1985* – This was carried out by US bombers in direct response to the support for international terrorism provided by Colonel Gadaffi, the Libyan leader. However, many civilian areas of the city were hit. The episode only served to harden Libyan opinion against the United States and cause tensions between doves and hawks in the European Union.

Abu Nidal

Nidal is seen as one of the most notorious terrorists of the twentieth century. He masterminded many atrocities since his early entry into the Palestine Liberation Organisation, a group which he left in 1974 to found the Fatah Revolutionary Council, a rival organisation. Nidal has received sponsorship at different times from Iraq, Syria and Libya, and has carried out specific assassinations, and attacks on Rome and Vienna airports. He has recruited only extremist Palestinians into his group.

1. What can we learn from Nidal's exploits?
2. Is modern terrorism more cruel, more indiscriminate?
3. Judging by current trends, from what areas or groups are terrorists most likely to come?
4. Are there other leaders who are typical of modern terrorists?
5. Is terrorism becoming the accepted method of warfare for the future?

Several factors appear to be promoting terrorism as a method of warfare:

▶ Terrorism is given the oxygen of publicity by the media. A one-minute slot on the early evening news about the victim, can also lead to a five-minute slot about the perpetrators.

▶ A growing number of states face disorder as a result of civil wars. To cover up economic and social shortcomings at home they may support terrorist violence abroad.

▶ Transnational terrorism and narco-terrorism can bring in vast profits. Helped by this, organisations such as the Palestine Liberation Organisation, have developed their own media channels and quasi-diplomatic representation abroad.

▶ Some people began as terrorists and freedom fighters and have become leaders in their own countries.

▶ The mere threat of nuclear, chemical or biological warfare can be viewed as terrorist blackmail.

The international development of terrorism

The Red Army Faction (Rote Armee Fraktion) is the oldest and most brutal of the terrorist organisations in Germany. It dates from 1970, and was formerly under the leadership of Meinhof and Mahler. It adopted a strategy of armed anti-imperialistic struggle aimed at destroying the imperialistic feudal system politically, economically and militarily.

With the support of other European groups it has taken international action against NATO forces. At a national level the struggle is conducted against the armed forces of the state apparatus which represents the monopoly of power of the ruling class. The group was opposed to the power structure of the multinational organisations the state and non-state bureaucracies, the parties, trade unions and the media. It has shown consistent anti-American feeling. Many lawyers have been attracted to the cause, keeping up links between arrested terrorists and those still operational. Violence is the propaganda of the deed. Members have had close links with the Irish Republican Army, Middle East terrorist organisations and Japanese groups. The Rote Armee Fraktion has proved the universal appeal of terrorism and that it is big business.

The kidnapping of James Cross

In October 1970 the British Trade Commissioner, James Cross, was kidnapped by the Quebec separatist organisation Front de Libération du Québec. A communiqué from the kidnappers demanded the release of 23 Front de Libération du Québec prisoners and their passage to Cuba or Algeria. They also demanded a large sum in ransom, the name of the informer who led the police to another cell in the organisation, publication of their manifesto and the cessation of police activity related to the kidnapping.

The federal government decided to meet one of the kidnappers' demands and broadcast the manifesto. It also agreed to provide safe passage for the kidnappers to a foreign country and clemency for the 23 prisoners if the victim was released. The other demands were refused.

A separate FLQ cell then kidnapped Pierre Laporte, the Quebec Transport Minister, and reiterated the original demands in full. Political confusion reigned. Some believed the kidnappers should be dealt with by the Quebec administration and accused the federal government of nullifying provincial authority. The federal government then invoked the War Measures Act, outlawing the FLQ and similar organisations and providing the police with powers to search without warrant. Over 200 arrests were made. Laporte was murdered by the FLQ and later, with Cuban help, an aircraft was made available for the kidnappers in return for the release of Cross. The terrorists left for Cuba, but the relations between the Federal and provincial governments were exacerbated rather than healed.

The operation demonstrated to the world that terrorists could carefully plan and execute their tasks, and in particular worried the Americans for whom the possibility of a destabilised Canada was not in their interest.

International humanitarian law and the rights of terrorists

International law is perhaps most useful as a measure of international concern and opinion on an issue such as terrorism. Such law cannot provide a direct answer to most questions raised by terrorism, simply because it is not applicable outside armed conflicts. The law unconditionally prohibits terrorist acts and provides for their repression. In peacetime, terrorist acts must and can generally be dealt with under the domestic law of states. The accused are entitled to humane treatment.

Each party is under an obligation to enact the necessary legislation to extend its criminal jurisdiction to any person who has committed a grave breach regardless of the nationality of the perpetrator, the victim or the scene of crime.

Terrorists not only violate the rights of others by violence, but they do so with the purpose of making everyone's rights insecure. Terrorists seek to destroy the community of understanding and mutual self-restraint upon which the existence of rights depends. A terrorist group alienates a population from its government by creating a sense of insecurity and provoking repressive measures.

In turn, terrorists jeopardise their own claims to human rights as they have murdered, tortured and violated the human dignity of their victims. Yet because the terrorist retains the distinctively human capacity to preserve life or seek death through his unique actions there has to be some relationship in law.

Do you therefore believe a terrorist has rights? Is international law vulnerable in relation to terrorism? In other words, can a general treaty on terrorism, undertaken by states with a common legal and political heritage, succeed where similar ones globally have failed?

Counter-terrorism

A fine balance has to be struck in trying to combat terrorism – too weak a response with under-equipped forces can be a disaster. At the other end of the spectrum, too zealous an approach to using forces can lead to the loss of lives. States have to fully support their counter-terrorist forces with intelligence and equipment.

Which of the following statements on counter-terror do you agree with and which reflects the assessment of the need for forces today?

1. Success in counter-terror depends on certain conditions being met. Planning is an essential prerequisite and lack of planning has led to more serious trouble than any other omission.

2. High levels of state coercion may be successful in suppressing violence by small groups as in South America in the 1970s, but these examples show how high the cost of the strategy of suppression can be. In Argentina and Uruguay, two examples of military rule and massive human rights violations, the cure was clearly worse than the basic problem.

Terrorism, intelligence and the law

All democratic countries have to face two areas of concern in fighting terrorism. Do governments use their intelligence-gathering purely to fight terrorism? How far does the media promote or reduce terrorism?

Decide what potential security concerns are in the following issues:

1. Too much coverage by the media of army and police tactics and strategy can only benefit the terrorists.

2. Violence is a form of communication, and may bring about compliance in the population.

3. Terrorist groups maintain that their actions are legitimate for political reasons and that what they do in fighting for freedom is not a criminal matter.

Crisis and risk management

Crisis management

Making a decision on how to protect the public and commerce and enforcing security systems is not easy. It is very hard for governments to manage crisis and risk in an effective way.

Crisis management teams should include individuals with the authority to put plans into action, and there has to be an effectively managed focal point. Verification of the level of threat is vital, followed by analysis and response.

No two negotiations with terrorists are alike, just as no two crises are alike. The keys to successful negotiations are a clearly defined strategy, knowledge of the opponent, experience as a negotiator and careful preparation.

Try to formulate a response to any of the terrorist issues raised in this book. How can you persuade sceptical organisations that success is vital?

Risk management

The task of risk management is to identify precisely the risks and probable effects of those risks on the personnel and organisation to be protected in the face of an ever present terrorist threat. The nature of the threat will determine the scope and structure for recommendations.

The important risks are property, legal and financial, personnel, physical, social and market. Each risk has to be measured by a number of criteria to determine its impact on the organisation. The results of the measurement determine how the risk is to be handled. In the case of acts of terrorism, which frequently involve the loss of life, risk avoidance, occurrence reduction and risk acceptance as means of risk management are the most important.

1. In risk and cost management, are there any different approaches to security which should be considered?

2. Do you think any management plan can cope with the rapid expansion in the forms and trends of terrorism?

Future trends

Which of the following statements on the danger of terrorism do you believe is most applicable in the current and future global environment?

1. 'The state sponsored terrorist and his patron can engage in acts of violence that are typically more destructive and bloodier than those carried out by groups acting on their own behalf.' (Hoffman)

2. 'The more isolated terrorists become from the world outside, the more likely it is that escalation and recklessness will occur.' (Drake)

3. 'Globalisation provides ideal conditions for the operation across state boundaries of small groups engaged in covert violence.' (Guelke)

4. 'Each terrorist has to be evaluated separately when we form policy.' (Wardlaw)

5. 'The future greatest potential problem of terrorism is technology. Technology can be used to enhance terrorist weapons; also modern societies are vulnerable to assaults on their technological facilities.' (White)

6. 'The problem of solving terrorism raises the insoluble problem of how to get good government around the world.' (Taylor, in Livingston ed.)

13

The Events of 11 September 2001 and Repercussions

One-minute summary – In this chapter we will examine the events of 11 September 2001 and the consequences for the world community. In particular we will explore:

▶ the action
▶ worrying aspects of the attacks
▶ the Taliban. Who are they?
▶ what these key terrorist groups hate
▶ fundamental and Islamist ideals
▶ the West and the crisis
▶ the effect of the crisis on the Irish troubles
▶ key terrorist groups under international scrutiny in 2001
▶ the military options
▶ financing terrorism
▶ economic implications
▶ asymmetrical warfare
▶ the next threat?
▶ globalisation of terrorism
▶ dilemmas facing the world community.

The action

The events which occurred on 11 September 2001 in the USA have been ascribed as the worst terrorist outrages in history. The events stunned a nation and shocked the world. Shocking, searing, awesome and horrid images were witnessed all around the world almost as they were taking place, through the medium of terrestrial and satellite TV, video, radio and e-mail.

The world was stunned into silence by the deliberate crashing of four US passenger planes, the first two at 08.50 and 09.08 into the North and South towers of the World Trade Centre in New York, causing all seven buildings in the World Trade Centre to partially or totally collapse. At 09.30 the third plane flew into the south-western section of the Pentagon (US defence headquarters) in Washington. At 10.00 the fourth crashed into a field in Pennsylvania (almost certainly bound for another high profile target). It is estimated that up to 5,000 people from over 80 nations lost their lives in the resulting devastation.

The date, like 7 December 1941 (Pearl Harbour, when 2,300 died) will live in infamy. It was the largest loss of American life in a single day since the Battle of Antietam Creek, Maryland on 17 September 1862 during the American Civil War when 23,000 were killed or wounded.

The audacious air assault on the political and financial capitals challenged the idea of Fortress America and ended the illusion that its citizens can somehow float above the hatreds of the world. The first World Trade Centre bombing on 26 February 1993 which killed 6 people and injured more than 1,000 might have been a powerful warning, especially when investigators discovered that the plotters had meant to topple the Towers and packed the truck bomb with cyanide in an effort to create a crude chemical weapon.

The immediate effect of the terrorist attacks of 11 September reverberated across the USA and led to the closure of:

▶ the Stock Exchange
▶ all airports
▶ all government offices in Washington
▶ major tourist sites such as Disney World.

Who was to blame? was the immediate cry.

▶ Was it the fault of the CIA and FBI for a failure of intelligence, especially as in midsummer some foreign intelligence agencies had warned of a possible terrorist attack in America?

▶ Could it be the work of Osama bin Laden, known for plotting earlier attacks against American military and diplomatic targets in Yemen, Kenya and Uganda, who was in Afghanistan and had survived a cruise missile strike by the Clinton Administration in 1998?

▶ Was it the Taliban in Afghanistan – the ruling party of Islamic extremist students in the country since 1994 who were known for harbouring terrorists? Their supreme leader, Mullah Mohammed Omar is especially hostile to the West – and is elusive (allowing no photos and never appearing in public).

▶ Were the Palestinians to blame? In spite of Yasir Arafat's shock, large numbers of Palestinians in the shanties of the West Bank and Gaza cheered the attacks.

▶ Was it Iraq? The state run media applauded the collapse of the Towers in New York and linked it to America collapsing.

Worrying aspects of the attacks

The following key points have emerged.

▶ Despite America's dominant role in world aviation, security at its airports has long been regarded as dangerously complacent.

▶ Minimal training appears to have been needed to fly an airliner, and there was apparent ease of getting onto the flight deck.

▶ There are no limits for the new breed of terrorist. Bin Laden has changed the rules with his blatant disregard for public opinion.

▶ To some Muslims who see America as the enemy of Islam the devastation in America was divine retribution.

▶ A wealthy businessman can control thousands of Arab militants – there are no financial barriers and the religious fervour is infectious.

▶ The mission of terror against the World Trade Centre was finally completed eight years after the initial outrage.

▶ Insurance claims will run into billions of dollars.

▶ The need to protect peaceful Moslems while rooting out the extremists, and maintain respect for individual Moslems, mosques and other institutions.

▶ Prejudicial statements may occur and should be avoided.

▶ Extra protection against acts of vandalism is needed.

▶ Support is vital from the media.

▶ Institutions which funnel Moslem youth into jihad (sacred war) must be opposed.

▶ There are Islamist 'sleepers' who go quietly about their business until one day they are called into action.

▶ The west must listen to advice of anti-terrorist Moslems.

▶ Specific, undesirable internet sites should be closed.

▶ We must heighten aircraft profiling – the practice of looking at passengers' ethnic and religious characteristics.

▶ Reconsider past mistakes.

The Taliban. Who are they?

Taliban means students of religion at special religious schools (*madrassahs*) and was formed as a militia in 1994 to quell the chaos that followed Soviet withdrawal from Afghanistan in 1989. They served the capital Kabul in 1996 establishing an Islamic emirate, but operate from Kandahar the country's religious centre.

They believe that women shouldn't work. Theft is punished by amputation. Idolating and proselytising are forbidden. Although they were initially popular because they improved order, they still face armed opposition and Bin Laden's fighters keep the Taliban on top. Taliban support is found among minorities in the neighbouring countries of Pakistan, Iran and Tajikistan.

Afghanistan is a country in ruins after over 20 years of war, and is one of the most wretched places in the world – the following figures show why.

- ▶ population — 26 million
- ▶ life expectancy — 43 years
- ▶ illiteracy — 75%
- ▶ annual GNP — capita $700
- ▶ refugees — 3.6 million, mostly in Pakistan and Afghanistan
- ▶ internally displaced — 500,000 to 1 million
- ▶ famine — 12 million affected by worst drought in three decades
- ▶ land mines — 6 million – 100 people killed/maimed each week.

The ethno linguistic groups

1. These are very complex. There are two ethnic groups:
   - *Iranian*: Pathan, Hazara, Aimak, Baluchi and Tajik
   - *Turkic*: Uzbek, Turkmen and Kirghiz.

2. The main linguistic groups are:
   - *Pashto* – the first official language is spoken by the dominant ethnic group, the Pathans
   - *Dari* – the second official language is used for inter-ethnic communication and is spoken by some Pathans and the Hazaras, Tajiks, Uzbeks and Turkmen.

These groups in some cases spill over into Pakistan which has an ethnic dilemma – and ethnic groups include Baluchi, Pathan (Pushtun), Punjabi and Sindhi.

The two groups likely to fight each other within the country for power are the Taliban and the Northern Alliance Jamiat-I-Islam, a coalition supported by the West who did have hope in the most efficient member Ahmad Shah Massoud – but he was murdered in

Afghanistan on 8 September 2001 by two suicide bombers posing as journalists.

What these key terrorist groups hate

Primarily they see America as the Great Satan and all its values as evil and infinitely inferior to their ideals. There are two groups:

1. Violent ideologues like Bin Laden.

2. Arab radicals including fundamentalists and secular nationalists.

The sources of Arab displeasure are:

▶ The American support of Israel politically, economically and militarily.

▶ Arab opinion also thinks that merely to protect its access to oil, the USA supports repressive crimes in the Persian Gulf states. The presence of American troops in Saudi Arabia is seen as a sacrilege to many Arabs.

▶ Many do not understand why the USA insists, ten years after the Gulf War, on worldwide sanctions that are devastating the Iraqi people.

▶ The Arabs resent that they are not seen as the geopolitical player they believe themselves to be, based on the historical expansion of Islamic power.

▶ Islamic fundamentalism has grown as a result of the effects of colonialism and western modernity. Such views are held even more strongly than the advance of Arab nationalism, especially as they are triumphalist religious convictions.

The groups see globalisation as yet another system that enriches the privileged and entraps the powerless – based not on envy but on genuine outrage about inequality.

Fundamentalism and Islamist ideals

Osama bin Laden, the Saudi dissident sheltering as a guest of the Taliban regime emerged as the prime suspect for masterminding the attacks. He has consistently denied involvement though he did offer his congratulations to the hijackers. Bin Laden has appealed to those in the religious colleges, where the extent of learning is a rudimentary form of Islam. These are the Taliban who have warred with brutality and ruled with a primitive absolutism. He has cemented his place with them and achieved a form of Islamic sainthood by supplying funds and hundreds of Arab fighters who have stiffened the Taliban at critical moments.

Bin Laden inherited at least $30 million and made millions more running the construction company founded by his father. He then entered Middle Eastern legend by abandoning his privileged existence for the perilous life of a Mujahed and was welcomed as a war hero.

▶ Saudi Arabia's connection to these terrorists is strong. Embracing Wahhabism, a rigid, puritanical version of Islam, the Saudi regime has tried to bolster its faltering legitimacy in the past two decades by fuelling a religious revival in the Arab world.

▶ Egypt has repressed political dissent. It censors information and opposition movements have been increasingly forced underground.

▶ In the Arab world, 65% of its population is under 18, it has stagnant economies and a fetid political culture. Thousands of young men with little chance of employment, are increasingly taking comfort in radical religious and political doctrines that promise salvation through a struggle with the West. They hate their own regimes as well as the outside world, for example the Al-Qaeda network began in the early 1990s as a series of desperate groups in Algeria, Egypt and Saudi Arabia and were seeking to topple their respective governments.

Bin Laden has no throne, no armies, not even any real

territory apart from Afghanistan; but he has the power to make men willingly go to their deaths for the sole purpose of indiscriminately killing Americans.

▶ Bin Laden, assuming he was responsible, has been able to puncture the American security bubble of homeland defence.

▶ Even if Bin Laden is neutralised, plenty of militant fundamentalists would be ready to struggle on in his name – with or without direct orders from their hero.

▶ Despite its apparent new ferocity and the outpourings of hate for the infidel from Bin Laden, Islam remains primarily a tolerant faith – for instance Jihad is not seen as a holy war by the moderates, but as striving to perfect oneself, or to give hope to others by good example.

The Palestinian struggle
▶ The Palestinian cause suffered as a result of the atrocity. Palestinian leaders disassociated themselves from the attacks in USA but sympathy for their cause appears to have declined.

▶ The Jewish cause was enhanced for, in their view, the atrocity showed how dangerous fundamentalist terror can be. Nevertheless, Israel is upset by the West's wooing of the Arab world to prevent other terrorist incidents.

The Palestinians' situation has not been helped the by members of Hamas and Jihad imploring to be sent to an early death – new assassins were queuing eagerly for martyrdom or suicide bombing. Hardliners in the Islamic world were said to be slow to condemn the hijackers.

The West in its turn has to look at its own security to make sure it is not used as a 'safe haven' by the terrorists. Western attitude will perhaps have to change if terrorism is to be defeated – political correctness in relation to human rights and individual freedom have become too much of an obsession.

The West and the crisis

1. In each western country, every government department went on a high state of alert, after 11 September 2001.

2. Advice is being given to nuclear installations and water treatment plants on how to combat attacks.

3. Intelligence sources began working to prevent the spread of nuclear, chemical and biological weapons.

4. Governments began reviewing emergency plans held by all their departments.

5. Attempts were being made to break down terrorist cells in the USA, UK, Spain, Belgium, Netherlands, Germany and Dubai where many believe the 11 September attackers had links. Up to 300 operatives of the Bin Laden network were planted in Europe.

6. Security was tightened, especially at airports. Measures included armed guards, cockpit door locks, comprehensive check-in procedures and regular stricter identification checks. There is constant monitoring of the Internet.

7. Checks were made on all possible sources for militant support for the Taliban – possibly from 20 nations.

There have to be some common agreements on extradition treaties between nations and how they can speed up the procedure. For instance European Human Rights law, incorporated into UK law in October 2000, precludes Britain extraditing any terror suspect to a country which has the death penalty. This obviously affects the UK/USA extradition treaty and has already caused anger in the USA. The UK has only agreed to return suspects if the USA waives its right to impose the death penalty. EU human rights lawyers support the USA against international terrorism but have a principle against the death penalty.

The effect of the crisis on the Irish troubles

The events of 11 September for Sinn Fein certainly opened a breach with the USA in terms of Irish Republicanism's 'peace strategy'. Republican sources believe the West's policy in the Middle East has been a disaster, and lashing out vaguely at targets defined as 'international terrorism' will fulfil only the desire for revenge and inflame the region.

Sinn Fein had received bad news before 11 September, when three alleged IRA men were arrested in Colombia in August 2001. They were accused of training the Marxist terrorist group FARC, a sworn enemy of the USA, in bomb making and of entering Colombia on false passports.

The appeasement of terrorism has certainly gone out of fashion. The USA is so concerned by FARC's potential to destabilise the region and its control of the cocaine trade, that it has committed millions of dollars and military expertise to fighting the insurgents.

The key terrorist groups under international scrutiny in 2001

1. **Al-Qaeda** is run by Osama Bin Laden and works with extremists seeking to overthrow all non-Islamic governments and expel westerners and non-Moslems from Moslem countries. The USA believes this group is ultimately responsible for the attacks on the World Trade Centre and the Pentagon.

2. **Algama'al-Islamiyya** is Egypt's largest militant group, and started in the 1970s. It seeks to overthrow the Egyptian government and eliminate the Coptic Christians. The group has supported Bin Laden and supports the killing of Western citizens. In November 1997 it attacked and killed 58 foreign tourists at Luxor in Egypt.

3. **Hamas** was born out of the outgrowth of the Palestinian branch of the Moslem Brotherhood in 1987. Ultimately it demands an Islamic Palestinian state in place of Israel. In 2001 it orchestrated suicide bombings of a discotheque and pizza restaurant in Israel, killing 39 people. Hamas is located

in the Gaza Strip and West Bank.

4. **Hizbullah** is a radical group opposed to Middle East peace negotiations and seeks more political power in Lebanon. It is anti-western and closely allied with Iran and Syria. In 1983 they perpetrated in the suicide truck bombing of US embassy and US Marine barracks in Beirut, Lebanon.

5. **Al-Jihad** is based in Egypt and targets Egyptian officials and US and Egyptian facilities. It has been active since 1970s and works with Bin laden. In 1981 it assassinated President Sadat of Egypt.

The military options

There are perhaps four options that one can consider in the immediate aftermath of the outrages.

1. **General air strikes** against Afghanistan which can be done by carriers in the Gulf but Bin Laden could escape, along with much of his terrorism planning staff.

2. **Bombing other** countries that help or shelter terrorists, not just Afghanistan. The wider the attacks, the louder the protests in the Moslem world.

3. **Invading Afghanistan** – this would destroy the terrorists, but it would require consistent help from Iran and Pakistan. Bin Laden could slip away.

4. **Commando raids** plus support for the Afghan resistance, by USA and NATO countries. This is the likeliest way of killing or capturing Bin Laden. In the longer term the anti-terrorism allies could arm and train the anti-Taliban Northern Alliance, even though the most prominent anti-Taliban leader, Ahmad Masoud, was killed (8 September 2001).

The status quo is not an option – but serious harm could be done to the anti-terrorist alliance on a global scale if many thousands of innocent civilians are killed. In the Arab world, powerful minorities can whip up mass demonstrations quickly calling for a Jihad or holy war against the USA and leading to the overthrow of even moderate Arab governments.

Financing terrorism

President Bush aims to stop Osama bin Laden, or anyone else, from financing terrorism. Most terrorist assets in relation to 11 September events are outside the USA and under disguised names. Assets of high profile individuals can be frozen or confiscated.

1. Money generated by criminal activities, notably drug trafficking, has been grabbed by the authorities.

2. The International Monetary Fund reckons that the amount of money being washed through the financial system is between $500 billion and $1.5 trillion a year – equivalent to 5% of gross world product.

3. In many countries (e.g. offshore financial centres) bank customers are protected by privacy and secrecy laws.

4. Terrorists moving money from regions that finance them to their target country are similar to those used by criminal gangs, for example, a deposit of dirty money is made in a bank with standing instructions to wire it on in small, random fragments to hundreds of other bank accounts around the world. Tracking down the money can take years.

The source of terrorist money can be legal (which cannot be said for money laundering) – it might come from a wealthy individual or a religious charity. Money starts off 'clean' becoming 'dirty' only when the terrorist crime is committed later on.

International cooperation is vital as money can be spread far and wide, across the globe.

Economic implications

The implications of the outrage to the American and world economies are vast and far reaching.

1. Insurance claims alone could reach $30 billion or 1% of annual growth for wrecked offices, telecommunications, displaced workers and of course the victims.

2. The stock markets were down and the US economy heading for recession even before the events.

3. The profits of the world airline industries have nosedived.

4. Tourism declined markedly from early September 2001.

5. Financial firms who occupied the World Trade Centre have been devastated and the loss of intellectual acumen will affect the US economy.

6. The collapse of retail activity – 11,000 businesses were affected.

7. The damage in Manhattan itself (which accounts for 2.5% of overall US GDP).

8. The psychological effects of people not wishing to do any work/trading in the wake of such an enormous tragedy.

9. External investors wonder if Wall Street can come back.

10. Fifteen million square feet of office space has been lost or severely damaged, plus 75,000 phone lines and 19,600 miles of phone cable. Full redevelopment of the site of the World Trade Centre could take a decade.

To cause economic breakdown has always been one of the tenets of those who practice revolutionary conflict.

Asymmetrical warfare

This was born on 11 September 2001 as far as the USA was

concerned. Asymmetrical warfare is the capacity of those who lack the money and high technology of the United States to wage what amounts to war, to deploy intelligence, ideology and low technology against the greater power, therefore the 'rogue states' are now a much greater threat to the free world than any old-fashioned power bloc.

▶ The USA cannot counter such methods by the conventional projection of its massed might. It needs to be smarter.

▶ Over the past decade or so, predictions have been made that militant Islam and western democracy will clash. The clash will asymmetrical and therefore heavily biased in favour of the West. To many observers the Moslems are reduced to terrorism simply because they are poor.

▶ The USA was targeted on 11 September, because two ardent peoples – Arab and Jew – are fighting an irreconcilable war over a single piece of territory and the USA is backing one side.

▶ What must worry the USA, is that planning for the outrage started in 1999 at flying schools in Florida where many of the 19 terrorists, including 7 pilots who took part in the atrocity, were trained. Their countries of origin were Egypt, Saudi Arabia, United Arab Emirates and Lebanon.

▶ The terrorists were divided into two groups – those assigned to flying lessons and those given logistical or support roles. They trained primarily on how to use digital instrument cockpit simulators.

▶ The terrorists believed they could mingle in with other ethnic groups and the Arab-American population – over 56% coming from Lebanon and of the total number of Arab-Americans 42% are Catholic and 23% Moslem.

▶ The United States froze the assets of 27 names including 11 organisations, 13 individuals, two charities and one company. The organisations are active in Algeria, Egypt, Kashmir, Lebanon, Libya, the Philippines, Uzbekistan and Yemen. Six are already banned in Britain. Accounts are

being examined in the Isle of Man, Gibraltar and
Switzerland.

▶ There are fears in America that the terrorists' next outrage
could be detonating bombs or lorries carrying dangerous
chemicals. Several individuals apparently linked to the
hijackers have fraudulently obtained or attempted to obtain
hazardous transportation licences.

▶ In October 2001 three people contracted anthrax in Florida,
one of whom died and this has sent a wave of new fear even
though there is no evidence of a link with the outrages.
Officials have launched a criminal investigation into the
source of the disease, and this appears the more likely
scenario. The American mail is currently being targetted.

The next threat?

Until 11 September 2001 no terrorist group had carried out so
complex a mission. The three main types of weapons of mass
destruction – **biological agents**, **nuclear bombs** and **chemical
weapons**, now have to be reassessed as a threat.

1. *Chemical weapons* – the raw materials for weapons such as
   powerful nerve toxins are relatively easy to get, but they are
   not well suited for inflicting widespread damage. To kill a
   sizeable number of people with sarin (which can be absorbed
   through the skin as a liquid, or inhaled as a vapour) one would
   need a crop-dusting plane, hence the compounding of such
   planes in the USA. To attack a city with sarin would not be
   easy as many thousands of tons are needed. The non-military
   chemical attack by the Aum Shinrikyo cult in Tokyo in 1995
   killed only a dozen people, as the amounts of gas used were
   small.

2. *Nuclear weapons* – to undertake such an attack a terrorist would
   have to get hold of a fissionable substance such as enriched
   uranium – but even if it could be obtained from new states of
   the former Soviet Union, it would take 70 kg of uranium plus

hundreds of kilos of casing and machinery to make a weapon. The greater fear is an attack on a nuclear power plant with conventional explosives.

3. *Biological weapons* – possible agents include anthrax and smallpox – both are potentially lethal. During the Cold War both sides developed anthrax as a biological weapon and today quite a few nations have biological weapon pro-grammes. Water supplies could be affected by contaminating reservoirs.

The cyanide bomb attack by Saddam Hussein's forces on the Kurdish village of Halabja in 1988 with its resulting mass deaths serves as a reminder to us all of its massive destructive potential.

The terrorists' game is to wage war and not be seen, and this is possible with this particular aspect of warfare.

The key issues

▶ The panic effect can be vast, especially if the target is a large civilian population.

▶ Even a small amount of chemical (as used on the Tokyo underground in 1995) caused great fear.

▶ Biological and chemical attacks can turn against the perpetrators.

▶ Antidotes can be produced, e.g. to nerve gas.

▶ Agents' shelf life can be reduced by adverse weather.

▶ The methods of delivery needed to cause huge casualties have to be large scale and, therefore, more noticeable.

Globalisation of terrorism

1. The events of 11 September 2001 in New York and Washington ushered in the beginning of a new and uncertain struggle.

2. Terrorism has been globalised – a few terrorists like Bin Laden

are big, well financed and organised.

3. Terrorists in today's global village need money, banks, telecommunications, transport facilities and local assistance.

4. Terrorists need other organisations, even governments, to help them.

5. The greatest single threat faced is low-tech, high intelligence terrorism both at home and abroad. This is likely to have more repercussions than trying to build a missile shield against intercontinental ballistic missiles. Former potential enemies in the Cold War and its immediate aftermath – Russia and China – have of necessity come round to the western way of thinking on these matters.

6. Counter-terrorism needs huge funds as well as worldwide support and there is a need to shore up a vitally important aspect of counter-terrorism – covert operations.

7. The world of globalisation is the outcome of policies and values that the USA and western democracies have adopted for decades or centuries. The West has created a world in which individuals are free to choose how they would like to live their lives – how they work, travel, trade, worship, organise, speak and think. These issues are deeply threatening to the world view of Osama bin Laden, extremists and revolutionaries.

8. The USA is the pivot that makes today's globalisation go around and this has been put under threat.

9. The global coalition began to come together in October 2001 – with the vital ingredient of exacting support or non-resistance from pivotal states in the Middle East.

10. For the first time in its history the North Atlantic Treaty Organisation invoked its mutual defence clause article.

11. European Union leaders backed the validity of an American response and said member states were ready, each according to its means, to engage themselves in such actions.

12. The United Nations could invoke a Security Council resolu-

tion for military action but any excessive strike could inflame the Moslem world, in which there are 1 billion people forming a majority of the population of 45 countries.

13. The attacks on 11 September were an attack on globalisation. Tyrants and terrorists see global capitalism as a threat to their power. In the eyes of the terrorist, globalisation stands for cultural dominance, the rapid growth of the super rich and western modernity – all areas which they utterly abhor or reject. Universal civilisation is anathema to the terrorist.

Dilemmas facing the world community

► The war on terrorism must be waged on a mode of behaviour, not on a particular enemy.

► The harder one strikes back at the terrorists, the more thousands of 'Bin Ladens' will be created.

► The momentum of the current Islamic fundamentalist revival – one of a number witnessed in world history, has been gathering pace at least since the 1950s.

► Is the war about terror, or about Islam? Many perhaps have the uncomfortable realisation that it will become more about the latter.

► Islamophobia has exacted a brutal toll in reprisal for Islamic violence – a fact often forgotten. Examples are:
   – the shooting down by the USA of an Iranian airliner in July 1988 over the Gulf
   – the assassinations carried out by Israelis
   – the attacks in Moslem-dominated Chechnya by the Russians in response to bomb outrages in Moscow
   – the hanging of Islamists in Xinjiang province in China by the Chinese
   – the near genocide of Moslems in Bosnia.

► Millions have fled the Islamic world and in the 1990s some three-quarters of the world's migrants are said to have been Moslems. They have been escaping:

- sharia law
- inter-Moslem conflict
- economic chaos
- Moslem–Christian violence
- anti-Moslem aggression.

▶ Escapees, victims, scapegoats, malefactors and 'sleepers' await their call to jihad and what they believe to be Paradise. Refugees, migrants and asylum seekers will increase and be seen as a threat by many western countries if of Middle East origin.

▶ In a war of civilisations, would the West prevail?

▶ In a war against terrorism, is it ethical to drop food packs at the same time as bombs?

▶ Bin Laden appeared very effectively on an Islamist TV station in the Gulf (Al Jazeera). Should western leaders respond (as has happened) with interviews countering his comments or does Bin Laden win the propaganda war?

Tutorial

Progress questions
1. Why was Afghanistan at the centre of the 11 September 2001 crisis?

2. Why do Islamic fundamentalist groups hate the West?

3. How are terrorist groups financed?

4. What is meant by the term 'asymmetrical warfare'?

5. What are the key dilemmas facing the world community in how to deal with terrorism?

Discussion points
1. Why is Palestine's future seen as the key to ending the current international terrorism crisis?

2. How is the crisis resulting from the World Trade Centre

atrocity affecting the future of Northern Ireland?

3. Is biowarfare really a credible part of the terrorist's arsenal?

4. How can the fight against Osama bin Laden and Islamic fundamentalist terror be genuinely seen as not a 'crusade' against Islam as many in the Arab world see it?

5. Is the dropping of food parcels at the same time as bombs really effective, genuine and credible?

Practical assignments

1. Outline a plan for the eradication of world terrorism that is realistic and effective. How, if at all, does your plan vary from the ones currently being undertaken by the West?

2. How can Israel and the Palestinians be persuaded that the recent events have focused on the need for a solution to the long-term impasse of sovereignty? What can be done to breathe new life into the peace process?

3. In what ways can long-term military options be dovetailed into continuing diplomatic options?

Appendix 1
Simulation and Gaming in the Study of Conflict

The advantages of simulation exercises and gaming techniques

Simulation and game-playing exercises are useful in the development of problem-solving skills, negotiation skills and the understanding of conflict theory. With their use the dynamics of terror and the complex policy and value issues which terrorism raises can more easily be understood.

1. Students are given a chance to manage many of the policy issues surrounding terrorism. In conjunction with macro and policy objectives, students can express their own personal views on the issues raised by terrorism.

2. Attention can be focused on the impact of terrorism and its counter-measures on the democratic character and civil liberties of our society.

3. Students can be challenged to respond to tendentious assertions such as 'one of the reasons why terrorism is a virulent poison is that the cure can damage society as much as the disease'.

4. In order to have a value-focused discussion, students must work through a simulation and read some of the scholars who have faced the dilemma in their own work. Students thereby learn about opposing perspectives on terror and are provided with a means to test out their reactions to these issues, a task of primary importance.

The conduct of simulation can result in the following advantages:

▶ Students have a greater understanding of the causes of violent civil disturbance.

▶ Students are afforded an opportunity to express themselves in speech and writing. By dealing academically with the subject they are able to put theory into practice.

▶ Students will gain a broader experience similar to that acquired through an independent research organisation. Ongoing research and study will be encouraged allowing detailed projects to be undertaken on terrorism. The results of the simulation can be distributed to interested parties.

Conduct and outcomes of a simulation or gaming exercise

Simulations and games have links with role-playing. The parties concerned are represented by teams and most players have specific roles. The goals can be political, economic, military or judicial. The documents required include a resource file and a strategic political plan. The outcomes include:

▶ Continuation of the status quo.

▶ Negotiations leading to a negotiated settlement.

▶ The development of a crisis.

▶ The failure of negotiations, leading to a crisis.

▶ The failure of negotiations, leading to the continuation of the status quo.

▶ The success of negotiations, leading to the implementation of agreements.

During the simulation students will be advised by knowledgeable instructors representing a panel of experts. Pre-simulation preparations will also be required. For example, to study the Middle

East a consideration of the roots of the Arab–Israeli positions and the attitudes of the opposing sides, the Palestinian problem and the involvement of the superpowers and other major powers will be essential.

The simulation itself includes:

▶ an evaluation of the knowledge acquired

▶ the conduct of decision-making processes

▶ an exploration of modern diplomacy

▶ a consideration of the role of the mass media in political processes.

Ultimately a comprehensive and complete picture of the forces and factors in world events is built up. At the same time students gain experience of the use of analytical tools.

Debriefing terrorist games

The response should be based on your own experience in the terrorist game. One suggestion is to fill in the empty spaces in a list, such as the one given below, with a phrase or sentence:

▶ General factors for terrorists.....................................

▶ General factors for authorities ....

▶ The question of amnesty was ....

▶ The role of the hostage was ....

▶ The role of the media was ....

The following types of question should also be answered as true or false. The rationale for your decision should also be given.

▶ The progress of negotiations as perceived by terrorists and authorities. Each side will put their own interpretation on this issue.

▶ The 'other side' used media to their advantage and our disadvantage.

▶ 'Our side' showed flexibility in negotiation.

▶ 'Our side' attempted to use positive symbolic acts to scale down tension levels.

While scenario writing is in favour among the uniformed services it can have drawbacks. For example, the chain of imaginary events may seem plausible and unavoidable, whereas in revolutionary politics both sides can make mistakes. The object of the scenario is merely to offer a benchmark against which real situations can be tested.

Some observers are sceptical about the educational value to be obtained from the use of exercises by the uniformed services. There are, however, fewer misgivings for students taking part who are likely to become journalists, media people, law enforcement officers or government officials who may one day actually find themselves faced with the dilemmas raised in the games.

Students should be encouraged to research the literature in the bibliography. A discussion can then be initiated to produce a clear set of values:

	Strongly Agree	Agree	Disagree	Strongly Disagree
1. Control over the media must be exercised by government if terror is to be controlled.				
2. The safety of hostages should always be a primary concern when negotiating with terrorists.				
3. The Israeli approach to Entebbe in 1976 ought to be a model for our own nation in dealing with terrorists who take hostages.				

Class responses can be tabulated to maintain the discussion. After seeing how their own response pattern fits that of the whole class, students can be assigned a detailed essay on the rationale underlying their choices and to give them experience of how to deal with criticisms of their opinions raised in class discussion.

Suggested scenarios for use in simulation and gaming

1. Special advisers are brought to the Foreign Office on an emergency basis to make recommendations on a grave crisis: 'Early today a British diplomat, some of his family and his personal secretary were kidnapped in Algeria.'

    (a) Students are to make policy recommendations as to how to handle the problem. A day is allowed for delivery and reporting recommendations which will be subsequently passed to the Prime Minister.

    (b) Students get extra background information on the situation and the rules of the game before they complete the exercise.

    The exercise stimulates discussion on such issues as:

    ▶ the problem of deviating from previous policy when negotiating with terrorists;

    ▶ moral issues raised by various policy options;

    ▶ the input of various policies on the domestic and international environment.

2. A head of state has been seized. During a disarmament conference in the General Assembly Hall of the UN in September 1991, President Bush of the USA and the Soviet Foreign Minister were captured just outside the building by US White supremacists and Puerto Rican nationalists. They used a well thought-out and well executed plan of action and completely overran the building. Ten terrorists held over 100 people hostage (some escaping out of windows and back doors) plus over 50 delegates to the disarmament conference.

The Swiss government was called in (the Swiss delegate managed to escape the terrorists) as neutral observers and arbitrators as Switzerland is not a UN member.

The exercise is intriguing in its presentation of the problem of coordinating the policies of the USA and Russia. The game is also successful in teaching bargaining and negotiation skills.

3. Hijacking simulations can be excellent devices for dramatising the conflict between groups seeking a negotiated solution. They provide experience of a more tactical or action-oriented solution to an incident. Also covered is the freedom of the media during terrorist incidents and the development of a sense of camaraderie between the terrorists and hostages (the so-called Stockholm Syndrome).

Any international hijacking simulation can be run, or alternatively a role-playing exercise can be conducted in which a group of campus terrorists seize a building and hostages.

The success of such simulations in terms of the development of students' bargaining skills or sensitivity to particular issues is related to the quality of the debriefing exercises. Some suggestions for debriefing include:

▶ A videotape of the simulation may be replayed to illustrate misperceptions and distrust in the negotiations and terrorist/hostage rapport.

▶ Students may be required to conduct further research between the conclusion of the exercise and debriefing. For example, books on the topic of bargaining with airline hijackers may be consulted. This will provide a frame of reference based on conflict and bargaining theory for students to use in discussing what happened in their own role-playing experience.

▶ A class debriefing may be initiated. For example, all participants in the exercise complete a checklist of factors designed to pinpoint differences in attitude and perception.

Appendix 2
The World Wide Web and Terrorism

In the years before the world wide web came into existence protest groups were actively using:

▶ discussion lists (listeners);
▶ bulletin board system (BBSs);
▶ news groups (alt. Activism, militia, alt. Society, anarchy).

Today the Internet is widely used as a tool for protest groups in five ways:

1. The inexpensive and potentially broad access to millions of people allows protest groups to present propaganda explaining their position to people who are passive and uncommitted or just 'dropping by'.

2. The Internet provides information to like-minded people about specific topics of concern. It allows people who might never have met otherwise to communicate with each other about topics that anger them.

3. The Internet allows angry protest groups to level written attacks on the objects of their anger. Persons who are targets of a protest group's written venom may be subjected to these diatribes.

4. Protest groups can use the internet to request financial assistance from the general public.

5. The Internet can be used to perform acts of terrorism.

The Internet is ideal for use as a propaganda machine. The uncategorised selection provides a number of examples in a very general manner about some of the issues covered in the book. Readers will need to use the net and web in far greater detail than can be covered in these pages.

▶ Protest groups can proselytise potential members because so many people have access to the information, e.g. White Force supremacists in Chicago: http://www.stormfront.org/watchman/index.html.

▶ Propaganda can try and show readers they have been deceived into a complacency (false consciousness) that threatens to destroy them: http://www.geocities.com/CapitolHill/1781

▶ Seizure of the Japanese ambassador's residence in Peru: http://burn.ucsd.edu/ats/mrta.htm

▶ For communication between terror groups the Cause Web page is used: http://www.cheta.ret/cause

▶ Terrorists themselves are concerned that world control freaks could move to crush this situation: http://207.15.176.3.80/cause

▶ Texas secessionists tried a few activities and some of their members were arrested. A message was put out for their release: http://www.rapidramp.com/Users/marine/rmtaken.htm

▶ Aryan resistance groups in the USA have a page advertising their company at: http://www.resistance.com/founder.html

▶ Support activities are vital to garner funds for a cause, e.g. the Alpha Race supremacist group: http://www.alpha.org

▶ The Peru Shining Path group has a web site where supporters seek to export the revolutionary message: http://www.csrp.org/index.html.

▶ Counter-terrorism on the web site is vital, e.g. the Oklahoma City bomb: http://www.execpc.com/warning/dogpound.htm

▶ The future of cyber-terrorism, where the biological and virtual worlds converge, is explored at: http://ww.acsp.urc.edu/OICJ/CONFS

The fight against environmental terrorism provides a good

example of the variety of web sources available:

▶ Tackling environmental terror by destruction and violence: http://abc-news.go.com:80/section/science/DailyNews/ protest990120.html

▶ 'Underground', an animal liberation movement in Europe: http://www.animal-liberation.net/

▶ The Earth Liberation Front: http://abcnews.go.com/sections/us/dailyNews/elf981022.html

▶ Western States Center which monitors trends in Western USA: http://www.epn.org/westernstates/extreme.html

▶ 'Support eco-warriors' in the UK: http://www.enviroweb.org/nocompromise/features/ supportall.html

▶ 'The EcoTerror Response Network' works to bring about a legal crackdown on such terrorists: http://www.eskimo.com/~rarnold/ecoterror.html

▶ Environmentalist role: http://members.aol.com/Jwaugh7596/Green_Terror.html

▶ Radical environmentalists' attacks on industrial sites: http://capitalismmagazine.com/1998/sept/ecoterror.html

▶ Environment and global issues: http://www.globalideasbank.org/BI/BI-137.HTML

▶ Earth Liberation Front and industrial tourism: http://abcnews.go.com/sections/travel/DailyNews/ tourism_environment981026.html

▶ Terrorism Zone; http://adcenter.ZineZone.com

Further information on terrorism and related topics may be obtained from the following web sources:

▶ Check out what others say about terrorism at eGroup.com. The site is easy to browse and has over 250,000 entries: http://www.egroup.com

▶ Global Terrorism Decoded: http://www.globalterrorism

▶ Terrorism Research Center provides a series of essays,

documents and research papers online:
http://www.terrorism.com/

▶ Patterns of global terrorism, according to US government assessments may be found at: http://www.usis.usemb.se/

▶ Security Resource Net's Counter Terrorism, Terrorism Legislation and Executive Orders: Effective counter-terrorism information may be found at: http://nsi.org/

▶ Global Terrorism Decoded index.html is the only site on the web that offers original interviews on terrorism, by academics and military and security experts: http://www.globalterrorism.com/

▶ For anti-terrorism, counter-terrorism and protection – you have to think like a terrorist to defeat a terrorist: http://www.millenniumbeyond2000.com/

▶ Anti-terrorism related information: http://www.blkbox.com/

▶ Terrorism/weapons of mass destruction: http://wchd.neobright.net/

▶ Collection of articles and news updates on counter-terrorism and its methods: http://www.ict.org.il/

▶ Terrorism – bibliography covering American texts: http://www.towson.edu/

▶ International relations: general resources index on terrorism (Yahoo), information and archives: http://www.cfcsc.dnd.ca/

▶ Index: patterns of global terrorism in the wake of recent terrorist threats to the US with security on the minds of many Americans planning international trips: http://scout7.cs.wisc.edu/

▶ Terrorism defined at a variety of different sources: http://www.bcpl.lib.md.us/

▶ The counter-terrorism headline list is a new offering from the counter-terrorism page: http://www.terrorism.net/

▶ Terrorism links – from the diplomatic and security viewpoints: http://www.cdt.org/policy/terrorism/Center for Democracy and Technology http://www.heroes.net

Appendix 3
Suggestions for Assignments, Projects and Research

Assignments

1. Produce a scenario based on any book on terrorism, e.g. Sterling (1990).

2. Write a counter-claim to the *Urban Guerrilla* mini manual.

3. Draft exercises as for a special course on terrorism.

4. Outline measures to capture a region or city by insurgency.

5. Write a case study of an individual terrorist.

6. Plan an anti-terrorist insurgency operation.

7. Write a calendar of terrorist activity.

8. Construct a major analysis of an area beset by terror, e.g. Ulster, the Basque Country, Turkey.

Projects

1. Conduct a series of book reviews.

2. Analyse a particular terrorist or terrorist group.

3. Make a comparison of different terrorist leaders at work.

4. Compile a list of revolutionary events analysing in depth the phases of subversion.

5. Prepare maps of major areas of conflict.

6. Describe how to conduct an anti-terrorist/counter-insurgency operation and form relevant legislation.

7. Form a revolutionary planning group and demonstrate how to bring about a deterioration in law and order.

8. Prepare a major exercise on Northern Ireland – include questionnaires, aims, method, preparation material; role play; the drawing up of topics to include in a conference to solve any particular situation.

Research

Using any summarised source of daily events such as Keesings, research the following in any singular calendar year.

1. Five acts of terrorism committed by national governments. Who declared these state acts to be 'terrorist'?

2. Five acts of terrorism committed by non-state groups. Who declared these acts to be 'terrorist'?

3. For each act in 1 and 2 briefly classify:
    (a) the most identifiable cause of terror;
    (b) the justification the 'terrorists' provided for their act;
    (c) the response of other political actors to the terror act.

4. Are there identifiable linkages between 'state terrorism' and group terrorism in the acts you have examined? If so, in what ways are the events related.

Tips

Study tips

1. How effectively do you make notes in words, patterns, diagrams?

2. Critically appraise the way you extract information from a book.

Revision tips

1. How do you best revise a detailed set of notes?

2. Be consistent in revision – never just read without making notes and comments.

3. Set yourself an essay based on the text you are revising.

4. Summarise your notes section by section on index cards, and use different coloured pens and writing styles (capitals, underlining).

Examination tips

1. Carefully plan each examination question and how you will use the time available. You might answer with an introduction, the main themes and conclusion.

2. Keep calm, cool and collected – do not rush.

3. Make sure you have answered the question and the correct number of questions.

Bibliography and Further Reading

Alexander, Y. and Pluchinsky, D.A. (eds) (1992) *European Terrorism Today and Tomorrow*. London: Brassey's.

Al-Hassan, O. (1997) *Terrorism, Organised Crime and Drugs: Repercussions for National Security*. London: Gulf Centre for Strategic Studies.

Amnesty International Report (1996) London: Amnesty International Publications.

Anderson, J.L. (1993) *Guerrillas: The Inside Stories of the World's Revolutionaries*. London: HarperCollins.

Apter, D.E. (ed.) (1997) *The Legitimization of Violence*. London: Macmillan.

Barkun, M. (1996) 'Religion, militias and Oklahoma City: The mind of conspiratorialists', *Terrorism and Political Violence*, vol. 8, no.1.

Beck, A. and Willis, A. (1993) *Terrorist Threat to Safe Shopping*. Leicester University: Scarman Centre for Public Order.

Benyon, J. (1996) *Crime Order and Policing*. Leicester University, Scarman Centre for Public Order.

Bolz, F., Dudonis, K.J. and Schulz, D.P. (1990) *The Counter-Terrorism Handbook*. New York: Elsevier Science.

Brown, D.J. and Merrill, R. (1983) *The Politics and Imagery of Terrorism*. Seattle, WA: Bay Press.

Carmichael, C.J.C. (1983) 'Of beasts, gods and civilised man; the justification of terrorism and of counterterrorist measures', *Terrorism*, vol. 6. pp. 1–26.

Central Intelligence Agency (n.d.) *Guide to the Analysis of Insurgency*. Washington, DC: US Government Printing Office.

Chalk, P. (1996) *West European Terrorism and Counter Terrorism, The Evolving Dynamic*. London: Macmillan Press.

Cilluffo, F.J. and Johnston, R.J. (1997) 'Doomsday cults: managing an unconventional threat', *International Police Review*, vol. 39.

Cornish, P. (1997) 'Sabotage by sarin: the threat of terrorism and weapons of mass destruction', *Intersec*, vol. 7, no. 9.

Daily Telegraph September, October 2001.

Dewar, M. (1992) *War in the Streets. The Story of Urban Combat from Calais to Khafji*. Newton Abbot: David & Charles.

Dewar, M. (1995) *Weapons and Equipment of Counter-Terrorism*. London: Arms and Armour Press.

Dillon, M. (1995) *Ireland, Twenty Five Years of Terror*. London, Bartam Books.

Drake, C. J.M. (1990) *Terrorism Target Selection*. London: Macmillan.

Durham, M. (1996) 'Preparing for Armageddon citizen militias, the patriot movement and the Oklahoma bombing', *Terrorism and Political Violence*, vol. 8, no. 1.

Elagab, O.Y. (1995) *International Law Documents Relating to Terrorism*. London: Cavendish.

Gearty, C. (ed.) (1996) *Terrorism*. Aldershot, Dartmouth.

Gearty, C.A. and Kimbrell, J.A. (1996) *Terrorism and the Rule of Law*. Oxford: Oxford University Press.

Gilmore, W. and Scott, A. (1997) *European Policy Responses to International Organised Crime*, Europa Institute Occasional Paper 3. Edinburgh: Edinburgh University Press.

Goldstone, J.A., Gurr, J.R., and Mashiri, F. (eds) (1991) *Revolutions of the Late Twentieth Century*. Oxford: Westview Press.

Gordon, A. (1996) 'Terrorism and science, technology and medicine databases: new concepts and terminology', *Terrorism and Political Violence*, vol. 8, no. 1.

Guelke, A. (1995) *The Age of Terrorism and the International Political System*. London and New York: IB Taurus.

Harmon, C. C. (2000) *Terrorism Today*. London: Frank Cass.

Harris, P. (1997) 'Algerian election puts democracy against terrorism', *Jane's Intelligence Review*, vol. 9, no. 9.

Hill, M. (1995) 'Beating the bombers', *The Police Review*, vol. 103.

Hocking, J. (1993) *Beyond Terrorism: The Development of the Australian Security State*. St Leonards, NSW: Allen & Unwin.

Hoffman, B. (1998) *Inside Terrorism*. London: Victor Gollancz.

Hoffman, B. (1997) 'The confluence of international and domestic trends in terrorism', *Terrorism and Political Violence*, vol. 9, no. 2.

Holland, J. and McDonald, H. (1994) *INLA Deadly Divisions*. Dublin: Torc.

Jamieson, A. (ed.) (1994) *Terrorism and Drug Trafficking in the 1990s*. Aldershot: Dartmouth.

Jamieson, A. (1997) *Collaboration: New Legal and Judicial Procedures for Countering Terrorism*. London: Research Institute for Study of Conflict and Terrorism.

Jenkins, M. (1980) *The Study of Terrorism: Definitional Problems*. Santa Monica, CA: Rand Corporation, p. 6563.

Jin-Tai Choi (1994) *Aviation Terrorism*. London: Macmillan/St Martin's Press.

Joes, A.J. (1992) *Modern Guerrilla Insurgency*. Westport, CT: and London: Praeger.

Kash, D. (1996) 'You can run but you can't hide: using RICO to fight terrorism', *The Police Journal*, vol. 69.

King, C. (1997) *Ending Civil Wars*, Adelphi Paper No. 308. International Institute of Strategic Studies, Oxford: Oxford University Press.

Kollen, K. (1984) *On Terrorists and Terrorism*. Santa Monica, CA: Rand Corporation, N-1942-RC.

Kushner, H.W. (ed.) (1998) *The Future of Terrorism*. London: Sage.

Livingstone, N. C. (1982) *The War against Terrorism*. Toronto: Lexington Books.

Lupsha, P.A. (1996) 'Transnational organised crime versus the nation state', *Terrorism and Political Violence*, vol. 2.

McDonald, W.F. (1995) 'The globalisation of criminology: the new frontier is the frontier', *Transnational Organised Crime*, vol. 1.

Maguire, K. (1995) 'Policing and counter insurgency in the Basque country', *Police Journal*, vol. 68, no. 5.

Moore, T. (1996) 'The fight for an independent Corsica', *Intersec*, vol. 6, no. 10.

Natanyahu, B. (1995) *Fighting Terrorism*. London: Allison & Busby.

Neuburger L. de C. and Valentini, T. (1996) *Women and Terrorism*. London: St. Martin's Press.

Nuthall, K. (1997) 'Call in the experts', *International Police Review*, vol. 39.

O'Ballance, E. (1996) 'Terrorism and intelligence', *Intersec*, vol. 6, no.11/12.

O'Ballance, E. (1997) *Islamic Fundamentalist Terror 1979–1985. The Iranian Connection*. London: Macmillan.

O'Neill, B.E. (1990) *Insurgency and Terrorism Inside Modern Revolutionary Warfare*. London: Brassey's.

Paletz, D.L. and Schmid, A.P. (eds) (1992) *Terrorism and the Media*. London: Sage.

Patrick, J., Ryan, I., and George, E. (1997) *Understanding Organised Crime in a Global Perspective: A Reader*. London: Sage.

Post, J.P. (1990) 'Terrorist psycho-logic: terrorist behaviour as a product of psychological forces', in W. Reich (ed.), *Origins of Terrorism*. Cambridge: Cambridge University Press.

Potter, K. (1995) 'Lens support', *Police Review*, vol. 103.

Potter, K. (1996) 'Fishy business', *Police Review*, vol. 104.

Presler, U. (1997) *An Institutionalised Solution to a Worldwide Epidemic*. Defense and Foreign Affairs Strategic Policy.

Purver, R. (1997) *Chemical and Biological Terrorism*, Conflict Studies No. 295. London: Research Institute for the Study of Conflict and Terrorism.

Reeves, S. (1999) *The New Jackals: Ramzi Yousef, Osama Bin Laden and the Future of Terrorism*. London: Andrew Deutsch.

Reich, W. (ed.) (1990) *Origins of Terrorism: Psychologies, Ideologies, Theologies, States of Mind*. Cambridge, Cambridge University Press.

Reid, K. (1997) 'Terrorism: Businesses and the Prevention of Terrorism (Additional Powers) Act 1996', *Journal of Financial Crime*, vol. 4, no. 3.

Robinson, B. (1997) 'Security risks and their management in British pharmaceutical industry'. MSc Thesis in Security Management, University of Leicester.

St Andrew's University (1996) 'Terrorism chronology for 1994', *Terrorism and Political Violence*, vol. 7.

Schmid, A.P. (1996) 'The links between transnational organised crime and terrorist crimes.', *Transnational Organised Crime*, vol. 2, no. 4.

Smith, B.L. and Damphouse, K.R. (1996) 'Punishing political offenders: the effect of political motive on federal sentencing sivisions', *Criminology*, vol. 34, no. 3.

Smith, B.L. and Morgan, K.D. (1994) 'Terrorists right and left: empirical issues in profiling American terrorists', *Studies in Conflict and Terrorism*, vol. 17.

Smith, B.L. and Orvis, G.P. (1993) 'America's response to terrorism: an empirical analysis of federal intervention strategies during the 1980's', *Justice Quarterly*, vol. 10, no. 4.

Sonal, A. (1994) *Terrorism and Insurgency in India – A Study of the Human Element.* London: Lancer Publishers.

Sprinzak, E. (1995) 'Right-wing terrorism in a comparative perspective: the case of split deligitimisation', *Terrorism and Political Violence*, vol. 7.

Sterling, C. (1990) *The Mafia*. London: Hamish Hamilton.

Sunday Telegraph September, October 2001.

Taylor, M. and Horgan, J. (eds) (2000) *The Future of Terrorism*. London: Frank Cass.

Taylor, P. (1993) *States of Terror*. London: BBC Books.

Thackrah, J. R. (1987) *Encyclopaedia of Terrorism and Political Violence.* London: Routledge.

Thompson, L. (1994) *Ragged War: The Story of Unconventional and Counter-Revolutionary Warfare*. London: Arms and Armour Press.

Thompson, (1996) 'The IRA saga continues', *Intersec*, vol. 6, no. 10.

Venter, A. (1997) 'Iran still exporting terrorism to spread its Islamic vision', *Jane's Intelligence Review*, vol. 9, no. 11.

Waddington, P.A.J. (1993) *Trouble with Public Order. Police Perceptions of, and Response to, Types of Public Order Operation*. Reading University Centre for Study of Criminology.

Walker, C. (1992) *The Prevention of Terrorism in British Law*. Manchester: Manchester University Press.

Walker, C. (1996) 'Anti-terrorism for the future', *New Law Journal*, vol. 146.

Wardlaw, G. (1990) *Political Terrorism*. Cambridge: Cambridge University Press.

Whittaker, D. J. (ed) (2001) *The Terrorism Reader*. London: Routledge.

Wilkinson, P. (1986) *Terrorism and the Liberal State*. London: Macmillan.

Wilkinson, P. (ed.) (1993) *Technology and Terrorism*. London: Frank Cass

Wilkinson, P. (1994) 'Terrorism', in M. Foley (ed.), *Ideas that Shape Politics*. Manchester: Manchester University Press.

Wilkinson, B. (1996) 'The role of the military in combating terrorism in a democratic society', *Terrorism and Political Violence*, vol. 8, no. 3.

Yiu-Kong Chu (1995) *International Triad Movements the Threat of Chinese Organised Crime*. London: Research Institute for Study of Terrorism.

Zulaika, J. and Douglas, W.A. (1996) *Terror and Taboo: The Follies, Fables and Fates of Terrorism*. New York and London: Routledge.

Index